M000281639

Reforming the Unreformable

Reforming the Unreformable

Lessons from Nigeria

Ngozi Okonjo-Iweala

The MIT Press
Cambridge, Massachusetts
London, England

MIT Press books may be purchased at special quantity discounts for business or sales promotional use. For information, please email special_sales@mitpress.mit.edu or write to Special Sales Department, The MIT Press, 55 Hayward Street, Cambridge, MA 02142.

Set in Palatino by Toppan Best-set Premedia Limited. Printed and bound in the United States of America.

Library of Congress Cataloging-in-Publication Data

Okonjo-Iweala, Ngozi.
Reforming the unreformable : lessons from Nigeria / Ngozi Okonjo-Iweala.
    p.   cm.
Includes bibliographical references and index.
ISBN 978-0-262-01814-2 (hbk. : alk. paper)
1. Nigeria—Economic policy.   2. Nigeria—Economic conditions—1970–
3. Corruption—Nigeria.   I. Title.
HC1055.O3924   2012
339.509669—dc23
2012008453

10 9 8 7 6 5 4 3

for Adaora "the Adorable," so she might know Nigeria

Contents

Preface

Incorrigible. That's what everyone called Nigeria in the early 2000s. Unreformable. Hopeless. The nation was riddled with corruption, bloated with debt, battered by economic volatility. The macroeconomy was seriously imbalanced. A series of national institutions—the civil service, pensions, customs—were broken. Health care, education, and other basic services were poorly delivered. Infrastructure was in disarray or disrepair. Poverty was rampant, and inequality was deep.

This is what President Olusegun Obasanjo inherited when he came to office in 1999 during a transfer to democratic power after decades of military rule. In 2000, in those early days of democracy, he invited me to return to Nigeria, my home country, to serve as Economic Adviser to the President, specifically charged with cleaning up Nigeria's messy debt profile and establishing a Debt Management Office. I returned to Nigeria to serve as the country's Minister of Finance from 2003 to 2006, and then for a few months as Foreign Affairs Minister. It seemed, in those days, as though we had to fix everything at once.

Our first order of business was to establish credibility, fairness, and social trust. We needed Nigerians and foreigners to believe in the nation's government, so they would invest in the country and lend to it. We needed to redress fundamental inequality, pervasive corruption, and power struggles that were undermining Nigerian society.

This is a story of how we began implementing a series of solutions and set out to reform "unreformable" Nigeria. The lessons I learned during this time remain valuable for a wide range of countries—certainly for low-income oil-exporting countries, such as Nigeria, but also for any developing country struggling with its own set of problems and interested in the political economy of reform, and also for developed countries that must cope with volatility, large macroeconomic imbalances, or overborrowing.

The first two chapters cover how Nigeria's Economic Team laid out a comprehensive, multi-pronged strategy for reform. Our prime goals were reducing macroeconomic volatility and fighting corruption. To address various structural features of the Nigerian economy that hindered private-sector enterprise, by promoting privatization, deregulation, and liberalization (chapter 3) and reforming civil service, trade and tariffs, customs, and the banking sector (chapter 4).

We were fully aware of the hurdles ahead. At best, we had four years (Obasanjo's second term) to implement any proposed reforms. We drew guidance from recent theoretical and empirical work in development economics, including a burgeoning body of work on the economic problems faced by oil-exporting developing countries.

Chapters 5 and 6 cover the most sweeping reforms Nigeria had to institute to restore growth and social trust. We had to fight corruption and enhance transparency in our economic and social spheres in order to convince Nigerians and the world that we were serious about reform (chapter 5). We had to obtain debt relief to give Nigeria breathing room to pursue other reforms, and to put the country on a more sustainable footing for the future (chapter 6).

The final two chapters evaluate the lessons we learned, look forward, and examine how the global economic contraction affected Nigeria.

This is a story of development economics in action, drawn from the front lines of economic reform in Africa. It is also a book dear to my heart. I wish to acknowledge the courageous men and women who undertook the struggle for a better life for Nigerians, by Nigerians. I would like to see the lessons learned carried forward by the next generation of Nigerians, and in the next wave of reforms. I hope to infuse readers around the world with a passion for democratization and reform.

I believe that great challenges present great opportunities, and that the chance to reposition an economy can be a springboard for steadier, more diversified long-term growth. That is a message that directly addresses today's financial and political headlines, as both developed and developing nations attempt to rein in debt, manage volatility in their economies, save for the future, and build credibility with debtors and investors. I hope this book will prove useful to readers who want to meet those challenges.

Acknowledgments

This book took me four years to write—far longer than I expected it to take when I resigned from the Nigerian government in August 2006 and joined the Brookings Institution as a Distinguished Fellow. I thought I would spend a year there documenting my experience implementing reforms in Nigeria. Two things stood in the way. First, I found I needed time to digest the experience, stand back, and look at it objectively before beginning to write. Second, a year later, by the time I felt able to begin writing and had worked on a couple of chapters, I rejoined the World Bank as Managing Director. My 16-hour work days and my travel left very little time for writing. Nevertheless, I managed to write on weekends, on holidays, in airplanes—in short, anywhere I could cobble together a few hours. But all this required constant encouragement and assistance from wonderful friends and colleagues. I thank Philip Osafo-Kwaako, Bardia Sassanpour, Brian Pinto, Vera Songwe, Liang Wang, Supo Olusi, Kingsley Obiora, and Bright Okogu, whose support with research, chapter reviews, and intellectual debate on the issues helped move me forward and to clarify issues. I also thank Zelena Jagdeo for her help with numerous revisions and rewrites. As one of the few people capable of deciphering my terrible handwriting, she did a great job.

I owe a debt of gratitude to two other people. My agent, Andrew Wylie, believed I had a story to tell. He waited patiently for four years, encouraging me every so often. Without Nancy Morrison, my wonderful editor, this book would not have been possible. Swift, gifted, and diligent, she made sure, chapter by chapter, that the book would be readable. I also thank MIT's impressive publications team, especially Paul Bethge, Emily Taber, and Jane Macdonald, for their patience and cheerful support.

Finally, I extend deep gratitude and love to my children, Onyi, Andrew, Uzo, Okechukwu, and Uchechi, and to my husband, Ikemba, who actively encouraged and supported me while I was writing the book, and put up with my writing on family holidays and weekends. In particular, my son Uzodinma Iweala, a physician and a writer, inspired me to push on. To my parents, siblings, and extended family, thank you for your love and support.

1   Setting the Stage for Reform

How do people called upon to reform the economy of their country and manage a turn-around begin? Where should they turn for guidance? Although many economics textbooks devote pages to the theoretical aspects of reform, there are no guidebooks, manuals, or toolkits on the process of designing and implementing an economic reform program in a difficult low-income country, such as my home country of Nigeria. Even if there were manuals or toolkits, countries' economic and political circumstances and other "deep fundamentals" such as cultures and ethnic and religious makeups can differ greatly, so that guides that might apply in one country might not work in another. But, I thought, surely there must be lessons learned from efforts to reform individual countries that would be relevant to those starting out on the path to reform. All this led me to think deeply about the circumstances that had led to current efforts at economic reform in Nigeria.

Nigeria has had a checkered political and economic history. It is Africa's largest country by population, with about 160 million people, more than 350 ethnic groups, and as many languages. It was cobbled together and colonized by the British in the nineteenth century. Like many other African countries, it won independence in 1960. It went on to put in place a parliamentary democracy akin to Britain's, with a prime minister, a president who was a ceremonial head of state, and a bicameral legislature. This era, generally known in the country as the First Republic, lasted from 1960 to 1966 and was marked by ethnic tensions (fanned by many of the country's leading politicians), by poor governance, and by corruption.

In a way that outsiders often fail to understand or fully grasp, Nigeria has always been complex to govern in a way outsiders do not often understand or fully grasp. British colonialists and Nigerian politicians regularly exploited ethnic, religious (Christian, Muslim), and regional differences to divide the country rather than to build a nation. As a result, tensions abounded in the early days of the country. These tensions led to a series of military coups in 1966–67 and ultimately to a civil war—the Nigeria-Biafra war. The Ibos from the southeast of the country felt they had borne the brunt of ethnic tensions that exploded in the north of the country after the 1966 coup, in which northern leaders were killed in a military coup largely led by Ibo officers. Thousands of Ibos were killed in rioting in the north. Ibos fled to the eastern part of the country, where they seceded as Biafra. The war lasted from 1967 to 1970, when hostilities ceased and the focus turned to reintegration, reconciliation, and reconstruction.

The coups and the war paved the way for almost three decades of military rule, interrupted only briefly from 1979 to 1983 when General Olusegun Obasanjo returned the country to civilian rule in the so-called Second Republic under President Shehu Shagari. The 1983 coup of General Muhammadu Buhari ensured that the military stayed in control of political power until the return of democracy in 1999 under President Obasanjo. The years of military rule were politically and economically disastrous for Nigeria. Institutions of state were severely undermined as meritocracy gave way to mediocrity. Corruption, already burgeoning under the early politicians, became entrenched under military rule, and a kleptocratic elite with a very limited vision of the future of the country came into being. That elite remains largely intact today, even under democracy, and may constitute one of the biggest stumbling blocks in the way of Nigeria's progress.

On the economic side, Nigeria was and still is a well-endowed country. With the world's eighth-largest population, it has a big domestic market—in fact, the largest in Africa. Before the 1970s, its economy was based mainly on agriculture, and more than 80 percent of the population lived in rural areas. It exported a substantial share of the world's cocoa, palm oil, groundnuts, cotton, hides, skins, rubber, and coffee. Along with these agricultural products and commodities, it also exported tin, coal, and other minerals.

Exploration for hydrocarbons began as early as 1907. In 1956, crude oil was discovered in commercial quantities at Oloibiri in the Niger Delta. This discovery opened up the oil industry to investment from multinational oil companies such as Mobil, Tenneco, Amoseas (now Chevron Texaco), and Agip. Production of crude oil in commercial quantities began in 1958 at 5,000 barrels per day (bpd) and reached 17,000 bpd by 1960 (NNPC 2008).[1] Both production and exports rose rapidly except during the Nigeria-Biafra war. By 1970, after the war, production had risen to 1 million bpd, and by 1974 (at the height of the first global oil shock) it had reached 2.26 million bpd. As of 2010, Nigeria was producing about 2.3 million bpd. Its reserves of oil amount to 37.2 billion barrels—the tenth-largest reserves in the world (OPEC 2011). Nigeria also has 5,110 billion cubic meters of natural gas reserves—the ninth-largest in the world (ibid.). In addition to the hydrocarbons, Nigeria has considerable undeveloped deposits of more than thirty solid minerals, including bitumen and tantalite.

The surge in oil production in the 1970s, in conjunction with the oil shock, had profound effects on the shape and structure of Nigeria's economy and also on its politics. A diversifying economy before 1970, Nigeria quickly turned into a monoculture economy based on oil. The surge in oil revenues was not managed properly, and the economy was awash with considerable liquidity (including in foreign currency) chasing too few goods. This quickly manifested in all the classic signs of Dutch Disease[2]—a sudden influx of foreign-exchange income that causes inflation and results in neglect of investment in other parts of the economy. Nigeria's currency, the naira, became overvalued. The terms of trade turned against agriculture because the high value of the naira, made it easier and cheaper to import agricultural products than to produce them at home. With the adverse policy impact on agriculture and its neglect, there was tremendous out-migration of young people—labor—from rural to urban areas, further compounding the problems of the agriculture sector. Agriculture as a share of the value of exports declined from 75 percent in 1965 to 3 percent in 2010. Oil became the predominant export, going from 25 percent of exports by value in 1965 to about 96 percent by 2010. In four decades, oil became the primary source of revenue for the Nigerian government, averaging more than 75 percent of government revenues on an annual basis.

In 1985–1987, when oil prices plunged to US$8–10 per barrel and Nigeria could no longer pay its bills, there was a brief attempt to reform the economy and change its direction. Under General Ibrahim Babanginda, a structural adjustment program was implemented with the support of the International Monetary Fund (IMF) and the World Bank. While it recorded some successes in terms of fiscal tightening, reform of import licensing, and freeing up some sectors of the economy to the private sector, the fiscal stringency introduced cut into spending for the education and health sectors, affecting the well-being of many citizens, young and old. The devaluation of the naira cut into the purchasing power of ordinary Nigerians and further alienated them from the reforms. With public hostility increasing, the Babanginda administration abandoned the reforms half way, thus undercutting their impact. The episode left a bad taste in the mouth of many Nigerians and made them leery of reforms.

The economy never quite recovered from the distortions introduced by the almost exclusive reliance on income from oil and the inability to translate this oil wealth into better living standards for the majority of the population. Oil money virtually destroyed the social and moral fabric of society. Corruption became rampant during the four decades of mostly military dictatorships, reaching its height during the rule of General Sani Abacha (1993–1998). The brief periods of civilian rule were no better in terms of corrupt behavior of top officials and politicians.

From the mid 1970s to 2001, Nigeria earned more than US$300 billion from crude oil. Yet over the same period Nigeria borrowed abroad unwisely and unsustainably, accumulating up to US$30 billion in debt to the Paris Club of Creditors. This debt became difficult to service, especially during times of low oil prices, as in the mid 1980s. Though a great deal of oil revenue and borrowed money was invested in much-needed infrastructure, education, and health services, a lot was wasted on "white elephant" projects. A prime example is provided by the Ajaokuta Steel Mills, where an investment of more than US$5 billion yielded no returns to the economy.

A significant part of the resources disappeared into the hands of top-level and middle-level public officials and politicians, most of it ending up outside Nigeria, deposited in foreign bank accounts or used to buy or invest in foreign assets. By 2003, the dawn of the second Obasanjo administration, the economy was growing more slowly than the population: while the economy was increasing at an average 2.5 percent per year over the decade, the population was growing at 2.8 percent per year. Inflation soared into the double digits, foreign reserves fell, public institutions were very weak, and the manufacturing sector operated at low levels of capacity utilization. The structure of the economy remained skewed in the direction of hydrocarbons. Unemployment was high, even among recent university graduates, and Nigeria's human development indicators were among the worst of the low-income countries. It was clear that something had to be done to turn the economy around, and the newly democratically elected President Obasanjo saw an opportunity to make a difference.

My introduction to economic reform in my country really began in 2000 when, at the invitation of President Obasanjo, I took a leave of absence from my job at the World Bank to return to Nigeria for six months to serve as his Economic Adviser. My remit was very specific: advise the president on how to manage Nigeria's debt so that the country could begin the process of seeking and obtaining debt relief from its largely Western group of official creditors, all members of the Paris Club.

I first met President Obasanjo in 1999, shortly after he won the elections but before he was sworn in as president. He had decided to visit important Western capitals to engage in discussions about Nigeria's problems and to share his vision and his agenda for the country's economic and social recovery from the "dead" years of General Abacha's dictatorship. His public relations adviser, Onyema Ugochukwu, a relative and a close friend of my husband, thought that he needed additional briefing on topical international economic issues of the time, as well as specific advice on how to approach Western leaders on issues of concern to Nigeria, such as lifting the country's debt burden and improving its image.

Onyema Ugochukwu phoned me one Saturday morning in March 1999 and asked me to put together a brief that would help President Obasanjo prepare for his proposed world tour. The brief I put together focused on Nigeria's most pressing economic problems, especially its debt, and on how the international community could contribute to solutions. In particular, I suggested to the president that he might make the case to the international community that their support to solve pressing economic problems in Nigeria would yield the country a much needed "democracy dividend" after decades of military rule. The president liked the brief and the notion of a "democracy dividend." He used the expression extensively throughout his term in office.

I met President Obasanjo in person when he came to the United States a few weeks later. In January of 2000, he requested that I return to Nigeria as his Economic Adviser for six months. My work in those six months focused on sorting out the extent of the country's most important financial liabilities (including its US$30 billion in external debt), on getting the seven different offices managing different parts of the debt to cooperate with one another so we could begin to reconcile figures, and ultimately on creating a national Debt Management office (DMO) to bring some clarity and rationality to debt management. This work laid the foundation for my return as Minister of Finance three years later.

Building an Economic Team

In 2003, President Obasanjo won a second term in office and decided to focus much harder on reforming Nigeria's faltering economy. He needed a modern and technocratic finance minister who was familiar with the fierce politics of the time. My name was suggested to him by Lady Lynda Chalker, a former International Development Secretary of the United Kingdom based on recommendations from two other reformers—Nasir El Rufai and Oby Ezekwesili—with whom I had struck a friendship during my short stint at home. Since President Obasanjo was already familiar with my work, I seemed a logical choice, so he rang up my boss—James Wolfensohn, president of the World Bank—to ask him to persuade me to resign my job as vice president and corporate secretary of the World Bank to become Nigeria's Minister of Finance.

When Jim Wolfensohn approached me, I was torn and conflicted on both a personal and a professional level. On the personal level, my financial situation was different than it had been in 2000 during my advisory stint at home. Then, I had been able to forgo some of my earnings and benefits to serve because we had only one child attending a university. By 2003, we had two, and a third getting ready to go, and the main question that my husband and I had to confront was how to manage all the financial obligations without going into debt if I went home to serve President Obasanjo. On a professional level, setting up the Debt Management Office had been an eye-opening experience and at the same time a fulfilling one. I thought this would be an unprecedented opportunity to serve my country again, with a new democracy in place and a president who seemed open to change. But I had also experienced firsthand some of the complicated politics of implementing reform. Even with an issue as technical as debt management, there were people who were vested in the status quo and did not want change. It seemed to me that reforming the management of the country's debt would be a picnic in comparison with the challenges I would face as a Minister of Finance. This time, virtually every aspect of the economy would have to be reformed. A comprehensive strategy would be needed to stabilize Nigeria's volatile macroeconomic environment, tackle endemic corruption, and redress various structural features of the economy hindering private enterprise. The country's woeful social indicators and abysmal delivery of basic services such as power, water, and transportation would have to be addressed. The prospects were daunting.

Surely designing and implementing such wide-ranging reforms could not be done by one person alone. Were I to accept, I would need advice on how to approach that enormous task. And accept I did, after two weeks of reflection and consultation with family members and friends, many of whom were opposed to the idea because they felt it was too great a risk to my professional reputation. Many felt that somehow, to quote one of my friends, "my reputation would be rubbished"—either by those who would be against me in government or others outside.

Jim Wolfensohn proffered a great deal of wise advice that tended to confirm my own feelings that this could be a unique opportunity to give back to my country. Because the World Bank had a rule mandating resignation for those accepting policy-making positions, I resigned from my position there once I had decided to accept the offer from Nigeria. The financial problems were sorted out by President Obasanjo's approach to the United Nations Development Programme (UNDP) to open a Diaspora Fund similar to the arrangement they had worked out for Afghanistan and other countries. Returning members of the Nigerian diaspora would be paid their previous salaries for a year or two until they could make adequate financial arrangements to take care of their existing obligations abroad. Several of us returning to Nigeria benefited from this fund, and it made a clear difference in our ability to return at short notice. The arrangement later became controversial. Referred to in the news media as the "dollar salary" saga, it was seized on and played up over and over again by anti-reform elements to imply that I was somehow less than committed to Nigeria because I was being paid more than the other ministers, and in foreign currency. Neither the circumstances in which I took the job, nor the fact that I was not the only official being thus paid, nor even the fact that it was a transitional arrangement and that I gave it up during my last 15 months of work got much play in the media.

As I contemplated the tasks before me, there were no manuals to tell me what to do, so I turned to someone who had just had some success in managing economic reforms. Amaury Bier, Brazil's former deputy finance minister, had just joined the Board of the World Bank as Alternate Executive Director after four years of implementing successful economic reforms under the Cardoso administration. Jim Wolfensohn suggested I talk to him. How did they do it? What practical day to day steps did they take?

The first piece of advice Amaury Bier gave me was critical. "You will need to form an Economic Team of like-minded people who can stick together to fight the tough battles," he emphasized. In Brazil, he had learned the hard way, a team was essential to bring different perspectives and expertise to the design of the reform program, but, more important, to help push through the cabinet the approval of proposed reforms. Without team members supporting one another in cabinet, important reforms displacing vested interests could easily be blocked, he emphasized. He also counseled that building team spirit and keeping the team working together would be important as the reforms began to bite, since some people would be interested in dividing the team and fomenting dissension. To avoid this, Bier urged, the team should meet frequently—at least once a week—to discuss progress and problems.

A second piece of advice Bier gave was equally important: there was need for a comprehensive strategy that would set out major challenges and the reforms needed to turn these around. In particular, it would be important to build in the sustainability of such reforms right from the start to avoid later reversals. One good tool was the enactment of legislation to underpin reforms.

Armed with this advice, I flew to Nigeria in May 2003 to discuss the scope of my job and to get President Obasanjo's agreement on the formation of a Presidential Economic Team. The president readily agreed to the team, noting that I would lead it and he would preside over it as chair. Working with him, colleagues and I came up with a list of twelve members (see table A1.1 in the appendix) representing the areas of expertise that various reforms would require. These twelve people—with expertise in macroeconomics, microeconomics, debt management, privatization, private-sector development, governance, anti-corruption measures, civil-service reform, and budget management—became the core of the team.

One appointment of particular importance (because he or she would have the ear of the president every day) was that of Economic Adviser to the president. We needed a sound macroeconomist—something Nigeria had not had in many years—who would reinforce the importance of the reforms. I nominated Charles Chukwuma Soludo, who later became a central bank governor.

As the reform process moved along and more diverse sectoral input was needed, the president increased the size of the Economic Team to 20 members. Not all of the team's members were in the cabinet. In fact, initially only four of us were cabinet members; several others sat in as observers. While the four of us were adequate to push certain major reforms with the help of the president, we faced challenges numerous times from the anti-reform elements in the cabinet. I believe the existence of what was seen as an elite and especially privileged group of reformers within government did not help our case, and set off tensions and jealousies with non-reform-team cabinet members that sometimes fed into a desire to block proposals relating to the reforms. This was particularly the case with some of the macroeconomic and structural reforms, as will be evident in later chapters. As members of the reform team, we probably also were not sensitive enough to the views of others, as we felt under attack almost all the time. We could probably have spent more time cultivating cabinet members who were not on the reform team and better explaining the reforms to them. This may have made life a little easier. Other than three or four of us, most team members did not know one another and had never worked together before. There was a need to build trust, team spirit, and a sense of shared purpose.

Meeting at least once a week helped some, but what helped most was making sure that each team member had a clear task on which he or she had to deliver, and that each member knew that that task was essential to the reforms. In turn, reforms were used as a foundation for debt relief. Keeping team members focused on the debt-relief goal was helpful to team spirit. Building the team was an ongoing challenge, and we had early trials. I used various means to keep team spirit going. We focused on early successes, such as jointly scoping out the reform strategy and making a winning PowerPoint presentation of that strategy to British Prime Minister Tony Blair and his team at a September 2003 meeting between him and President Obasanjo. Joint work and early successful presentations of proposed reforms to both Nigerian and external audiences gave the team confidence that it was proceeding in the right direction.

Despite these efforts, the team faced many challenges and tensions in keeping together, some of these stoked from outside. One early challenge occurred in July 2003 right after cabinet members had been sworn in. The president invited all the new members and other top officials and presidential advisers to a one-day retreat to explain his priorities and objectives for the administration and also to familiarize most of us who had never been in government with the main public service rules and imperatives. Most of the new members of the Economic Team were there. We sat close to one another in some kind of solidarity. The retreat was well under way when the president announced (completely out of the blue, to me) that he would be moving the Budget Office of the Federation, normally part of the Ministry of Finance, to the Office of the President, along with the new budget director, who was also a member of the Economic Team. I could hardly believe what I had heard, and turned to a team member to double check if I had heard correctly. It was already evident that drastic reform of the budget process and of budget priorities would be central to the reforms. It would be important to link such reforms to changes in the financial management system in the finance ministry. Removing the Budget Office was akin to ripping the heart from the chest. I felt that this would make major changes impossible to achieve and would furthermore deprive the Ministry of Finance of a central economic and political function. I was also in shock because the president had not discussed this with me. I thought, as the Minister of Finance, that he would at least mention such a major change to me, and maybe even ask my opinion of it. The fact that he had not done this was a major eye opener.

I felt two things. First, I could not be Minister of Finance with a major function removed. It would be a hollow job. I would be unable to complete the reforms I had come to Nigeria to complete, and therefore there would be no need for my services. Second, the president evidently did not trust me. Otherwise, why would he not even have mentioned such a momentous change? I was angry and confused. To shield my feelings from public view, I got up and left the meeting hall. Other members of the Economic Team followed me out of the hall in concern and solidarity. By the time I walked out, I had resolved to leave—surely it would be impossible to continue under such circumstances. I shared my feelings with the team members, and several of them said they would also quit in solidarity. It was indeed a sad moment—the team was about to disintegrate even before it had had a chance to perform. I told team members that I didn't want that to happen, and urged them to return to the meeting room so as not to create a scene. But I would not be coming back. I was off to write my letter of resignation, barely two weeks into the job. A couple of the team members asked me to hold off while they tried to resolve the issue with the president. But I was resolved to go. I felt very strongly that if this could happen barely two weeks into the job, then the president would be capable of making other critical decisions without my knowledge, and that could put the whole reform effort in jeopardy. Better to go now early in the game and let "sunk costs be sunk," as economists would say.

I returned to the room where I was staying to pack, and met my father, who had just arrived from my hometown, Ogwashi-Uku, for a meeting in Abuja. I explained the situation to him. He backed my decision, but asked me to wait for the next day so we could leave together. I went ahead and wrote my letter of resignation. I then called the president's office and asked if I could see him after the retreat. I was granted an evening appointment. I took my resignation letter with me and handed it to the president in an audience filled with tension. He flung the letter at me and said I was free to resign and leave. I took that at face value, thanked him, and left. I later found out that the flinging of the letter was a sign for me to apologize and withdraw my resignation, but I was as yet untutored in presidential mannerisms and probably still would have resigned had I known what the gesture meant.

That evening, several people came to see me and to put pressure on me to withdraw my resignation. I refused. At the same time, two important members of the president's inner circle—Principal Secretary Steve Oronsaye and Vice President Alhaji Atiku Abubakar—put pressure on him to reconsider and find a way out. The president asked me to come back to see him the next morning. I attended the meeting with my father for support. At that meeting, the president told me that he had decided that the Budget Office could stay in the Ministry of Finance but the budget director would be reporting to him. I thanked him profusely for being so gracious and asked if the budget director could report jointly to him and to me to make it possible for me to ask him to execute needed changes to the budget process. The president accepted, and I asked for this agreement to be captured in writing in a memo that I would draft for his signature. Interestingly, the president accepted and signed the memo the next day.

I felt both relieved and apprehensive. The apprehension came from many who told me this act of the president was highly unusual and out of keeping with his character and I would pay for it later one way or another. The incident also served as my first real introduction to the Nigerian press. Somehow the news of my resignation leaked and I was besieged by reporters. No minister in Nigeria ever resigns—they are sacked, and they usually find out through an announcement on TV or radio news. The media wanted to know if I had really resigned and the true circumstances of the resignation. I was surprised that the news had leaked and spread. With no coaching on how to handle this, common sense told me to say as little as possible. My typical line to the press was that whatever issue there was had been resolved and I had no further comment. This did not endear me to many in the media looking for a way to discredit the presidency.

Throughout the ordeal, members of the Economic Team stuck by me and provided support and encouragement. What could have been a damaging incident for the team instead served to draw us closer together. As a team, we learned lessons on how and when to stick together and support one another for the sake of the reforms. Team spirit remained high even under further challenging circumstances until toward the end of the administration, when there was a deliberate attempt to divide the team and our team spirit began to fray.

Mapping Out the Reform Strategy

Even before the reform team had coalesced, some of us who formed the core of the reformers had begun to brainstorm on a strategy that would encapsulate the reforms. Nigeria was really not short on strategies, plans, or visions. We had Vision 2010, which attempted to articulate a way forward for the country's development. But this vision was actually not successfully translated into a medium-term program that could be implemented and monitored. We knew that we had to produce a medium-term plan that would pass three tests. It needed a sound diagnosis of the country's socioeconomic problems; it needed to propose solutions; and it needed to translate the solutions into specific actions that would produce results and could be monitored. We also knew that, in view of skepticism in the country about reforms and change, we would have to achieve some early victories that would signal change. My training at the World Bank, where I had worked on many reform matrixes for a variety of low-income and middle-income countries, would come in handy.

The impetus for quick work on the strategy came from a meeting scheduled for September 2003 between President Obasanjo and British Prime Minister Tony Blair to discuss Obasanjo's quest for debt relief and for a return of public assets that had been stolen from Nigeria and lodged in the UK. The president had proposed that the Economic

Team accompany him to this meeting to explain Nigeria's proposed new economic reforms. I solicited written inputs from members of the Economic Team already working on important areas of reform—privatization, budget monitoring, and price intelligence linked to public procurement reform. For example, over a weekend, using their inputs, I produced a 17-page paper outlining the major economic and social problems and especially highlighting the problem of Nigeria's huge external debt overhang, which was a drag on investment and economic growth. I proposed a set of macroeconomic and structural reforms focusing on budget management and priority setting; fiscal reforms; liberalization and deregulation of important economic sectors; privatization of important public enterprises; governance and institutional reforms, including public service reform; and anti-corruption actions, especially concerning public procurement.

After completing the first draft, I invited comments and inputs from team members, then translated the paper into a PowerPoint presentation for the president's review and comment, including a set of matrixes of specific reform actions with a time line. I presented the plan first to a joint UK technical team from the Department of International Development and the Treasury, which wanted to make sure we had something serious to share with the prime minister, and then to the prime minister himself. Prime Minister Blair also invited World Bank president Jim Wolfensohn to the meeting to get his views on Nigeria's reforms. With a successful presentation, we knew we had the basis to deepen the analysis into a full-fledged program of change for the economy, incorporating action in essential sectors, including agriculture, education, and health. During that visit to the UK, the Economic Team stayed late into the night further debating the content and even the name for the strategy. We bandied various names around. It was Nasir El Rufai who came up with the name that we would eventually use for the strategy: the National Economic Empowerment and Development Strategy (NEEDS).

Back in Nigeria, the team decided that work on the strategy and actual implementation of reforms would have to move in parallel. We could not afford to wait to act until the strategy was deepened and completed. After all, we already had the essential elements of proposed reforms outlined in the strategy paper and captured in an action matrix and time line. Because NEEDS took a year longer to complete than had been planned (the process of crafting the strategy was very inclusive), this turned out to be a smart decision.

We agreed that a task manager was needed to lead the further development of NEEDS. Charles Soludo successfully argued that the Planning Agency (which he led in addition to his job as Economic Adviser) was the rightful place to lodge the preparation of NEEDS.

He also made two additional important points. First, it would be good to reach out to the academic community, the private sector, civil society, government employees, and other stakeholders and involve them in the task; the strategy should be seen as much as possible as a bottom-up as well as a top-down exercise, with as broad an ownership as possible. Second, we should think in terms not only of the NEEDS but also of SEEDs (State Economic Empowerment and Development Strategies) and even LEEDS (Local Government Economic Empowerment and Development Strategies). Nigeria's 36 states and 774 local governments controlled approximately half of government revenue and had a great deal of constitutional autonomy to spend it. Any reforms of a fiscal nature or improvements in the delivery of basic services would have to involve the decentralized entities. Getting their leadership on the same page in terms of strategy would be important.

Within NEEDS, we identified four central challenges responsible for the parlous state of the Nigerian economy and the impoverishment of the majority of its people. The first was poor economic management, underscored by the volatile pattern of public expenditure, and the monocultural orientation of the economy. The second was poor governance and weak public institutions undermined by ingrained and institutionalized corruption. The third was the inability of the state to deliver basic public services. The fourth was a hostile environment for private-sector growth, typified by bureaucratic hurdles and requirements.

To overcome these four challenges, NEEDS focused on four goals: wealth creation, employment generation, poverty reduction, and value reorientation. The latter goal sought to recall for Nigerians some of the traditional values that had long guided society and made corruption a thing of shame: respect for elders, honesty and accountability, cooperation, industry, discipline, self-confidence, and moral courage.[3] The point was that this new strategy for economic advancement should be built on our traditional set of values, toward which Nigeria's youth should be reoriented for a sound and sustainable future.

To achieve these goals, we proposed three actions. The first was changing the way government works by strengthening the management of public finances, better prioritizing expenditures, restructuring the bloated civil service, introducing transparency in government business, and fighting corruption. The second was promoting private enterprise as the primary engine of growth by deregulating and liberalizing important sectors of the economy and incentivizing the private sector to invest and create jobs. The third was empowering people by improving the delivery of basic services that matter for their lives—education, health, and essential infrastructure (clean water, sanitation, and so on). This also would entail investing in agriculture to create jobs, and supporting micro, small, and medium enterprises (MSMEs), which are the source of livelihood for a majority of Nigerians, especially women.

Our analysis showed that we would have to reach and sustain a minimum growth rate of 7 percent per year from 2007 to 2015 in order to succeed in cutting poverty in half—an objective we wanted to aim for in tandem with the internationally accepted UN Millennium Development Goals (MDGs). Anything less would mean stagnation or a worsening of the incidence of poverty.

While the NEEDS exercise was ongoing, many of the 36 states also embarked on the development of their SEEDS, tailoring each to the circumstances of the state but each having as a core the same goals and pillars as NEEDS. Most SEEDS included an analysis of state public finances and proposed actions to improve them, focusing on delivery of basic services such as education and health and on analyzing sources of growth in the state's economy (for example, in agriculture, manufacturing, and small and medium-size enterprises) through which growth could be enhanced and jobs could be created. By January of 2005, about a quarter of the states had their SEEDS completed or substantially under way.

Once the goals and the main pillars of action had been set out in NEEDS, the next step was to identify actual programs, tasks, and instruments to implement these actions. We built on earlier reforms that we were already implementing to carry forward to macroeconomic reforms (essentially reforms to public finances, including external debt, and to the fiscal and monetary policy regimes); structural reforms, including the whole area of deregulating and liberalizing major economic sectors and privatizing public enterprises, reforming the civil service and other important government services; and bringing transparency to government business, including specific actions to fight corruption. The rest of the book tells the story of the successes and failures of these various reforms.

The process of crafting and marketing NEEDS was unique in Nigeria's history. Never before had there been so much outreach to different segments of the community to put together an economic development strategy. The Economic Team, with the president's support and often with his participation, marketed the plan tirelessly to different audiences in the country so that even those who had not had a chance to make inputs into its development had a chance to offer their critiques. And there were *many* critics, including those who felt that the strategy had too much of what they termed a "neoliberal" Western flavor.

The strategy was also very comprehensive, and set many difficult targets for particular sectors. There were criticisms that the strategy was very ambitious, and indeed it was. But if the team could support, facilitate, and push for the most critical of these reforms, this would be an unprecedented achievement in the country's economic history. The team undertook countless road shows both within and outside Nigeria and made presentations to civil society, the private sector, and state and local government workers.

The document became a living plan adjusting to accommodate comments and critiques. By the end of the exercise, we could truly say that NEEDS was a homegrown Nigerian strategy and action plan to reduce poverty and create wealth—a plan put together by Nigerians for Nigeria. NEEDS was later vetted by the IMF and the World Bank to see if it could be accepted as Nigeria's Poverty Reduction Strategy Program (PRSP), a basic requirement of the two institutions for assistance to its poorer members (and one that they usually assist many countries with weaker capacities to prepare). Our plan was praised and accepted with no changes—an unprecedented act. I believe that the widespread awareness of NEEDS and the sense of ownership of this strategy by many Nigerians helped push through many of the economic reforms.

But there was great opposition to reforms, as will be seen throughout this book. The greatest opposition occurred in instances in which greater transparency was to be introduced into government business, because senior political and business figures were benefiting from the government's presence in these areas. Many attempts to restrict the government to its regulatory functions and get it out of activities in which it was evidently doing a bad job met with stiff resistance.

The Economic Team soon gained notoriety—or fame, depending on one's point of view—for demanding transparency in government business. Several of us were attacked continuously in the media and even physically threatened. Early in 2004, I received a phone threat from an anonymous male caller who told me to "pack up and go back to Washington" or else. Later the same year, my husband received a phone threat at his medical practice in Washington, DC, also from a male caller, telling him to withdraw me from Nigeria or else I would be killed. Shortly after this, a Nigerian woman who claimed to be an admirer of my work phoned my husband while visiting Washington and warned him to take precautions for my safety or else get me out of Nigeria because she had overheard two men on a flight to Lagos from Johannesburg threatening to "destroy me." My distraught husband insisted I report the threats to my safety to the president, which I did. My security detail was increased from two regular police and two Secret Service agents to four full-time Secret Service agents, and two extra mobile police to guard my house.

By this time, I had also earned a nickname in the press: "Okonjo wahala," which rhymes with my last name, Iweala. "Wahala" is a popular Pidgin English word in Nigeria meaning "trouble." So I was essentially nicknamed Okonjo the Trouble Maker. I loved this nickname and thought it was very creative. To me, it was a badge of honor. If I was regarded as "wahala" or trouble to the establishment because of my desire to clean up our public finances and work for a better life for Nigerians, then so be it. A trouble maker I would be.

2 Advancing Macroeconomic Reforms

On the morning of July 17, 2003, I sat down at my desk in Nigeria's Ministry of Finance, just after being sworn in with other ministers by President Olusegun Obasanjo as a member of the cabinet. I was overwhelmed when I reviewed the enormity of the problems confronting the country and saw the huge mountain of files already stacked for action on my desk. I wondered where to begin, and whether I had in fact been insane, as many friends and family thought, to leave my comfortable job and recent promotion to vice president at the World Bank to accept this huge challenge.

I had spent the two months between the time President Obasanjo first approached me to serve in May 2003 and the swearing-in ceremony in July working intensely on analyzing the problems of the economy and identifying the bottlenecks. This analysis clearly showed that if we were to make any headway in improving economic and social performance of the country, we had to begin with macroeconomic and budgetary reforms. We had inherited an unstable macroeconomic environment characterized by volatile exchange rates, double-digit inflation (23 percent on an annual basis in 2003), a high fiscal deficit (3.5 percent GDP in 2003), low foreign-exchange reserves ($US7.5 billion in 2003), and low GDP growth (2.3 percent on average for the past decade, including negative GDP growth per capita in those years because of the increase in population).

Essentially, our analysis showed that we faced two sets of problems. First, the economy was highly volatile, with loose fiscal policy and poor management of both the volatility and the fiscal policy. Second, there was no clear and consistent budgetary framework or budget process. The two sets of problems were strongly related—indeed, as we increasingly discovered, they were intertwined—and solutions had to be found for both. This chapter expands on the nature of the problems,

the solutions we found and implemented, and the visible progress that
came from this effort.

Nigeria—One of the World's Most Volatile Economies

Since the oil boom of the 1970s, the Nigerian economy has been highly
undiversified. The overwhelming share of exports (96 percent) and
government revenues (more than 75 percent) depend on oil. Oil
has two important attributes that demand attention and careful treatment. First, oil prices are internationally determined, highly volatile,
and unpredictable; hence oil revenues in any economy are highly
volatile. Second, oil is a depleting natural resource whose benefits
must be managed carefully for the good of both current and future
generations.

Economic management in Nigeria over the years had paid scant
attention to both attributes. Government expenditure in Nigeria was
volatile and procyclical: government spending rose in tandem with oil
prices and oil revenues, and dropped when prices crashed. The wide
fluctuations in government revenues and expenditures from 1971 to
2005 can be seen clearly in figure A2.1. Successive Nigerian governments had gone on a spending and borrowing spree during oil booms
in the 1970s, the early 1980s, and the 1990s that often resulted in poorly
planned projects of low quality, including such notable "white ele-
phants" as the Ajaokuta steel mill, on which $US5 billion was spent
and which produced virtually no usable steel. Spending sprees also
encouraged corruption, the bane of Nigeria's economy throughout the
years. A dismaying example was the cement import saga of the 1970s,
when the Nigerian government authorized the importation of millions
of metric tons of cement to support Nigeria's reconstruction effort after
the 1967–1970 civil war. Hundreds of millions of naira were spent.
Ships stayed lined up at the overcrowded harbor for months, unable
to offload, and incurring additional demurrage charges for government; later it was discovered that many of them were carrying loads
of sand.

Oil-price volatility and revenue volatility were made much worse
by Nigeria's loose fiscal policy. As oil prices increased, so did the
fiscal revenues that government could collect from oil, and so could
government spending; hence volatility in oil prices and oil revenues
translated into volatility in public spending, along with volatility in
exchange rates—with serious macroeconomic consequences. The

Nigerian economy earned the dubious distinction of being rated one of the most world's volatile. (See World Bank 2003 and table A2.1.) From 1961 to 2000, Nigeria ranked among the ten most volatile economies in the world on a range of macroeconomic variables, from terms of trade to per capita real GDP; indeed, it ranked in the top five for three of these variables. More important, Nigeria's volatility was more than twice the median volatility for almost all of these important economic variables.

Why does volatility matter? Because evidence shows that high volatility slows down productivity growth by a substantial margin, particularly in countries where the financial sector is insufficiently developed. Failure to manage the consequences of oil-price volatility, together with poor fiscal and exchange-rate policy, can lead to Dutch Disease. Nigeria's non-oil sectors, particularly agriculture, were classic victims of Dutch Disease during the oil booms. The high cost that volatility inflicted on the non-oil economy manifested in a precipitous decline in per capita non-oil real GDP growth from 1970 to 2003. (See figures A2.2 and A2.3.) The effect on social indicators was equally deleterious. (See table A2.2.) The effect of volatility on GDP growth is shown in table A2.3.

Despite its substantial oil earnings—estimated at US$300 billion since the 1970s—Nigeria remains mired in poverty, with high rates of adult illiteracy, maternal mortality, and infant mortality. It is expected to be one of the sub-Saharan African countries that will not meet the Millennium Development Goals by 2015. Infrastructure is poor. In a telling example, per capita consumption of electric power is low (121 kilowatt-hours) compared even to the average of low-income countries (317 kWh) and a fraction of consumption in South Africa (3,800 kWh). The challenge we faced—which may remain Nigeria's prime economic-management challenge—was managing oil-related volatility and ensuring that oil revenues would be spent to improve the lives of the Nigerian people.

What Did We Do to Solve These Problems?

Remember that Nigeria's oil earnings accounted for the lion's share of government revenues, and the fluctuations in those earnings were directly transmitted to the domestic economy through fluctuations in public expenditure. The simple way of addressing this problem would have been to de-link public expenditures from current oil revenues by adopting a fiscal rule based on the price of oil. This is what we did.

The Oil Price-based Fiscal Rule (OPFR) lets Nigeria escape from the tyranny of current oil prices by using a long-run average oil price. Nigeria adopted a reference price that mimics the long-run (10-year) average oil price. When actual prices rise above the reference price, the government can put away some of the excess revenues in the form of savings. When oil prices fall below the reference price, the government can draw on these savings to maintain its level of spending. This predictability is, in turn, imparted to the non-oil economy.

In 2004, when oil prices averaged US$33 per barrel, Nigeria adopted a reference price of US$25 per barrel to craft the budget. This generated savings of US$8 per barrel at a time when Nigeria was pumping an average of 2.3 million barrels of crude oil per day. In 2005, when prices averaged US$55 per barrel, Nigeria adopted a US$33 per barrel reference price. In 2006, when prices averaged US$60 per barrel, Nigeria boosted the reference price to US$45. A new Excess Crude Oil Account (ECA) was created at the central bank, and savings were held there and managed as part of the country's reserves. The savings were allocated to the three tiers of government of the Nigerian Federation (federal, state, and local), as stipulated in the constitution.

By the end of 2006, Nigeria had accumulated gross reserves of US$46 billion, of which US$8 billion were savings in the Excess Crude Oil Account *in spite* of utilizing US$12 billion in connection with the settlement of the US$30 billion Nigeria owed to the Paris Club. The OPFR was binding on all tiers of government. Thus it was not without controversy, as the states insisted that this was not constitutional. Some state governors declared that they did not see the need for this "rainy day fund," as I had termed it, since, given the development problems of the country and their states, they thought it was raining already—"in fact, the roof was coming down," as one governor put it. They argued forcefully that the money should be allocated for spending right away. We did a lot of jawboning to try to explain the volatility issue, and President Obasanjo courageously demonstrated the political will to hold the states to this agreement.

Successfully implementing an oil-price-based fiscal rule requires good timing relative to the trajectory of oil prices, and we were lucky. We began implementation of the rule when oil prices were on an upward trajectory, so savings could be built up in the first place. Nevertheless, successful implementation of an oil-price-based fiscal rule does not depend solely on building up savings. There are other factors. Let me make three observations.

First, although de-linking government spending from current oil revenues is a big step forward, it is not enough. The composition of spending also matters. Oil revenues are generated while a national asset, the country's oil reserves, is being depleted. That national asset belongs not just to the current generation but also to future ones. Thus, oil revenues should be spent on creating a springboard for stable long-run growth that will benefit future generations. This means spending the money wisely on long-term investments. Two types of investments are ideal: public investments in infrastructure to support diversified private investment in the non-oil sectors, and social expenditures in health and education.

Second, transferring oil revenues to the budget at the reference price must be accompanied by spending discipline. There is no point in accumulating savings when oil prices are high if government spending is out of control. This would be akin to a driver's putting one foot on the accelerator pedal and the other on the brake pedal. Spending discipline automatically puts a lid on borrowing and on debt accumulation.

Third, a fiscal system is needed that can facilitate and monitor the process whereby oil revenues are transferred to the budget, and can follow the subsequent spending and results. As I shall discuss in detail in the next section, Nigeria lacked a clear and consistent budget process.

Nigeria badly needed a medium-term macroeconomic program and a way of enshrining the OPFR in law to avoid backsliding. We dealt with those challenges by adopting a medium-term macroeconomic program supported by a new nonfinancial instrument the International Monetary Fund had just developed: the Policy Support Instrument (PSI). To instill fiscal discipline and tighten macroeconomic management, we designed a mix of fiscal and monetary policies in order to deliver macroeconomic stability in the medium term. We aimed at a fiscal deficit of 3 percent of GDP and a gradual reduction of the consolidated non-oil primary balance—the difference between the government's non-interest spending and non-oil revenues—from 41 percent of non-oil GDP in 2005 to 35 percent by 2006. We aimed to boost international reserves to reach US$26 billion by the end of 2005 and US$50 billion by the end of 2006 and to adopt tight monetary policies that would achieve single-digit inflation by the end of 2006. We invited the International Monetary Fund to support this program and monitor our progress through the Policy Support Instrument. This instrument allows the IMF to monitor a country and assist it in implementing a program without the country's having to borrow any financial resources. For us, it served as an external restraint that would be an additional support in implementing a tough set of self-imposed policies.

We next aimed to institutionalize the OPFR and fiscal discipline through the adoption of a Fiscal Responsibility Act. (See box 2.1.) In view of the controversy surrounding the OPFR and the lack of a budget framework and good budgetary practices at both federal and state levels, it became clear that a binding instrument would be needed to safeguard the macroeconomic reforms and lock in a good set of policies for managing volatility for the long term. A Fiscal Responsibility Act suited to a fiscally decentralized country such as Nigeria seemed to be the right instrument.

For inspiration on how to craft such a bill, we turned to another large fiscally decentralized country: Brazil. There was consensus at the federal government level that such a bill would be helpful. Nigeria's vice president at the time, Atiku Abubakar, and several lawmakers traveled to Brazil to learn about their bill. We subsequently adapted the Brazilian bill for Nigerian purposes, locking in adherence to the OPFR by all tiers of government and adherence to a fiscal deficit of no more than 3 percent of GDP over a three-year, medium-term expenditure horizon. We also locked in a requirement for an annual budget and for sound and transparent budgetary practices by the federal and state governments. We set limits to external borrowing for all tiers of government, including the terms for such borrowing.

Unfortunately, by the time the bill was passed and signed into law, near the end of 2007, state governments had watered down some of the provisions they found restrictive, using constitutional-related arguments. For example, the OPFR was retained, but with the proviso that the share of the savings belonging to state and local governments be released to them, while the share belonging to the federal government could accrue in the Excess Crude Account. In practice, though some savings have been shared from time to time, the federal government has largely resisted doing this. The wisdom of this restraint became clear during the global financial crisis of 2008–2010. When oil prices fell from more than US$140 to US$40 per barrel, Nigeria was able to draw on these savings to implement a modest fiscal stimulus equivalent to 0.5 percent of GDP.

Box 2.1
Landmark Legislation: The Fiscal Responsibility Act

In November 2007, after three years of consideration, the National Assembly approved and President Umaru Yar'Adua signed into law a landmark piece of legislation, the Fiscal Responsibility Act. It aimed to provide for prudent management of public resources, help ensure long-term macroeconomic stability, and support greater accountability and transparency in fiscal operations.

The Act sets out a general framework—the medium-term expenditure framework—that links policy, planning, and budgeting over the medium term (three financial years). The framework includes the following:

a macroeconomic framework setting out the macroeconomic projections
a fiscal strategy paper
an expenditure and revenue framework
a consolidated debt statement
a statement describing the nature and fiscal significance of contingent liabilities and quasi-fiscal activities and measures to offset such liabilities.

The framework commits all tiers of government to a set of rules for efficient economic management and set standards for the planning and control of public revenue and expenditure. By providing a debt-management framework and conditions for borrowing, including aiming for concessionality of borrowed funds, it seeks to ensure that government will not borrow and spend money without ensuring that it has the necessary funds to service debt. It sets general targets and limits for selected fiscal indicators for the country, with specific sanctions for noncompliance, such as sanctioning the finance minister.

The framework provides the basis for the annual budget and allocates resources to strategic priorities among and within sectors. It aims to ensure that annual revenue and expenditure estimates are consistent with its provisions through rules on cost and its control, budget execution and achievement of targets, and evaluation of program results.

The Act also aims at promoting transparency and reporting standards by facilitating parliamentary and public scrutiny of economic and monetary information and plans. It establishes the Fiscal Responsibility Commission to ensure that the provisions of the Act are properly followed through. The Commission is designed with the authority to compel any person and government institution to disclose information related to public revenues and expenditure. It can also initiate investigations on violations of the provisions of the Act and forward the investigation report to the appropriate authorities for possible prosecution.

Source: National Assembly of Nigeria, Fiscal Responsibility Act, 2007, Act No. 31.

Toward a Clear and Consistent Budget Process and Framework

As I mentioned, one daunting challenge we faced was the absence of a clear and consistent budget process and budget framework. Nigeria practices fiscal federalism through its federal structure, which is made up of the federal government, 36 states and the Federal Capital Territory of Abuja, and 774 local government areas. All revenues accruing to the Nigerian Federation—consisting mainly of revenues from oil and gas, from corporate and other income taxes, from the value-added tax (VAT), and from trade taxes—first go into the Federation Account and are then shared by the three tiers of government.

Before sharing, certain allocations are taken off the top of oil revenues. These include the cost of Nigeria's share of joint-venture production with various oil companies, which can range from US$2 billion to US$5 billion a year. A 13 percent derivation revenue is also taken off the top and directed to the six South-South zonal states in the Niger Delta as recognition that the oil revenues are "derived" from these states.

The remaining revenues are shared monthly according to a formula that allocates 48.5 percent to the federal government, 26.72 percent to the states, and 20.6 percent to the local governments, while the remaining 4.18 percent is allocated to Special Funds (including funds for the Federal Capital Territory) Against this allocation of revenue shares, the three tiers of government are supposed to prepare budgets outlining their priorities for expenditures. State and local governments enjoy a high degree of autonomy in the way their revenues are spent, as mandated by the constitution. State and local governments are nominally responsible for the delivery of such services as basic and secondary education, health services, and rural and state roads. In practice, the division of labor among the different tiers of government in service delivery has been murky.

The budget process that I encountered in the mid 2000s was ad hoc, opaque, and poorly planned. There was little coherence in budget formulation. Budgets tended to just repeat sectoral allocations from the past with some tweaking at the margin, perpetuating a legacy. Program implementation often deviated from the budget with impunity, as described in box 2.2. All this meant that the budget cycle created room for corruption and waste. To use a common Nigerian term, there were widespread *leakages* at various stages of the budget process. It was widely believed that one could bribe senior civil servants preparing the

Box 2.2
Nigeria's Neglected Budget Cycle

A normal budget cycle has four stages: budget formulation, a review process (typically by the lawmaking body, such as parliament or congress), actual budget implementation, and some monitoring of project execution.

In Nigeria, by contrast, the many years under military rule had eroded fiscal institutions and fostered an ad hoc budget formulation process without a coherent strategy to guide the government's spending program.

• Projects were selected simply to reward loyal constituencies or as favors for cronies. Multi-year projects were poorly planned; a project could be funded at inception, but then not funded in later years.
• The lack of a parliament meant that there was little oversight of public expenditure. A budget review process did not exist, and actual implementation of the budget was also a mess. When democracy returned in 1999, oversight from the National Assembly was restored, but the budget process was full of tension between the executive and National Assembly, as lawmakers tacked on many constituency projects, thereby bloating the budget and worsening the fiscal deficit.
• Release of funds was ad hoc and fraught with corruption, so that well-intentioned projects could suffer needless delays in implementation.
• When there were delays in financing the budget, there was a Ways and Means account at the central bank from which the government could borrow at will.
• Budget monitoring was nonexistent.
• Although each government department had a planning (or monitoring & evaluation) division, project supervision was at best superficial.

The whole budget process was marked by the absence of transparency. In many instances, the physical copy of the budget document was not even publicly available.

budget in order to get a desired project included. Monitoring and evaluation officials could also be routinely bribed to sign off on a shoddily completed project, or even on incomplete work. For example, a contractor building a road could cut costs by not building drainage systems or sidewalks specified in the project design. The government supervisor could simply ignore this and take his or her share of the "savings" accruing to the contractor. Moreover, because of poor record keeping between the Budget Office and the Accountant-General's office, millions of dollars could be lost when funds were being released to implement a project. In addition, the poor record keeping and lack of reconciliation of accounts routinely resulted in expenditures running ahead of revenues in a cash-based budget; thus, government institutions periodically accessed the Ways and Means account or overdraft facility at the central bank.

I was shocked to find systems in disarray and a very low level of computerization in both the Budget Office and the office of the Accountant-General of the Federation (AGF). Almost everything was handled through Excel spreadsheets. There were few links between the systems and the processes of the two offices.

The ministries, departments, and agencies (MDAs) that implemented the budget took advantage of this lack of coordination in various ways. Monies disbursed to the MDAs for operating expenses were routinely kept in accounts at various commercial banks, where favorable interest rates were negotiated by the senior civil servants responsible for oversight of these monies. While banks traded with the monies on their own account, top civil servants shared the interest that had accrued. There was no feeling that anything was wrong with this practice as long as the principal was untouched. As a result, monies were often kept in accounts for as long as possible to earn interest, while projects and programs went unexecuted. Sometimes ministers were unaware of what happened to the ministries' resources and complained in cabinet of a lack of resources for their programs, while the resources were lying idle in commercial bank accounts. Execution of the capital budget consistently fell below 50 percent and was at 24 percent in 2003. By 2003, the government had also accumulated arrears to domestic contractors amounting to about 150 billion naira (US$1.17 billion at the time).

I also found that there were no proper government records of these debts; they became another source of corrupt transactions that stretched out over the years as contractors were routinely asked by some unscrupulous budget officials for bribes when they brought in their receipts for validation and payment. Our initial attempts to audit and pay off these debts became a protracted negotiation between the Treasury and contractors as to how large the actual debts were. Over the years, pension arrears of parastatals, government agencies, and departments had also accumulated, reaching more than a trillion naira (the equivalent of US$8 billion at the time). Record keeping in this area was just as poor, and all combined to make for a fiscal nightmare.

Finally, there were structural problems with the budget—not least the fact that more than two-thirds of budget resources went for salaries and operating expenditures, leaving less than one-third for capital projects. Restructuring and reshaping a US$15–25 billion budget in the face of so many distortions and needs would prove difficult.

This problem was magnified at state and local government levels. Few states routinely prepared budgets. Citizens of most states were not even aware of the magnitude of resources collected by their state and local governments from the Federation Account, or of how much revenue was internally generated by the state (although most states, except Lagos, generated very little themselves and depended almost entirely on the allocations from the Federation Account). The lack of transparency of these accounts allowed corrupt appropriation of public monies to become a serious problem at the level of some Nigerian state governments.

What Did We Do to Improve the Budget Process?

To increase the efficiency of government spending and improve service delivery, we pushed for progress in the budget preparation process. We introduced three new planning and control tools: a fiscal strategy paper, a medium-term expenditure framework (MTEF), and medium-term sector strategies (MTSS). The annual fiscal strategy paper (FSP) outlined the federal government's anticipated expenditures and pro-jected revenue earnings. This was a broad strategy paper designed to enable the president and cabinet to make tradeoffs and determine budget priorities so that resources could be shifted in the priority directions.

The first fiscal strategy paper for the 2004 budget that I tabled for cabinet discussion in September 2003 elicited strong emotions and reac-tions from ministers whose sectors had not been given priority. This was the first time that tradeoffs were being made among sectors. Defense lost some allocations, while education and health expenditures were boosted—in the case of education by up to 50 percent. As a result, the "top brass" of the military demanded a meeting with the president. I attended that somewhat unnerving meeting. At the end of their pre-sentation, President Obasanjo, much to their chagrin, stuck to the pri-orities set out in the fiscal strategy paper.

I also recall that during a cabinet meeting I almost got slapped by the Minister of State for Women's Affairs, who felt hugely let down by what she thought were minimal allocations to her ministry. She had expected me—the first female Minister of Finance—to direct more resources to her ministry. In reality, I had agreed with the budget team that the most sensible way to empower women would be to "mainstream" assistance to women within the sectoral budget of each ministry, rather than make this a matter for Women's Affairs alone. But it took some time for the minister to internalize and accept this approach.

Once discussed and endorsed by cabinet, the fiscal strategy paper was circulated by the president to the National Assembly to give legislators a broad sense of the directions of the proposed budget. This was done to ensure that all parties in the budget debate could have a common understanding and literally be on the same page before the crafting of the budget began. The idea was to reduce the protracted debates and haggling once the budget was presented to parliament. The fiscal strategy paper had a measure of success in doing this, though the haggling and debates never quite ended. Starting with the 2005 budget, we also introduced discussion of the draft fiscal strategy paper with civil-society organizations to solicit their views and inputs as to priorities for the country and to involve them in the budget process.

Medium-term expenditure frameworks and medium-term sector strategies were also introduced to ensure that sectoral spending plans reflected existing government development priorities, and the proposed plans were in line with the projected range of resources for each government agency. The medium-term expenditure frameworks and medium-term sector strategies were three-year rolling budget frameworks. Each government ministry, department, and agency (MDA) was given an indicative resource envelope as a guide for its budget preparation. The medium-term expenditure frameworks and medium-term sector strategies ensured that government projects that spanned more than one year could be adequately budgeted for, with a clear plan for funding such projects over succeeding budget years. The adoption of both tools was important to keep projects from being abandoned, which was all too common in many parts of the country. These processes were also useful in compelling government agencies to make hard choices between using available resources to start new projects or complete existing ones.

A procurement process called the Due Process Mechanism was also introduced to reduce corruption and waste in government contracts stemming from inflated contracts. The Due Process Mechanism stipulated an open-tender process of competitive bidding for all government contracts and a value-for-money audit of contracts. Any project exceeding 50 million naira required formal approval by the

Budget Monitoring and Price Intelligence Unit (BMPIU). Once the budget was approved and passed into law, it was also important to ensure smooth financing of projects. I instituted a Cash Management Committee, which I chaired, to ensure that accounts were regularly reconciled between the Budget Office and the Accountant-General's Office and that Treasury had adequate funds to support timely quarterly releases for projects in the budget. To enhance transparency and increase the public's access to information, we ensured regular publication of the budget, both in paper form and on the websites of the Ministry of Finance and the Budget Office. A simple budget summary with highlights was also published to make the budget more comprehensible and accessible to the public. Budget monitoring was also improved with the publication of an annual Budget Implementation Report (BIR), essentially a review of the execution of selected capital projects. Teams of officials from the Ministry of Finance and from concerned sector ministries traveled around the country visiting a selected sample of projects from the investment portfolio to look at the quantity and quality of project implementation. Though not perfect, this helped to spur a jump in implementation and a concomitant rise in the utilization of the capital budget to 80–90 percent.

Implementation of some civil-service-reform measures—including weeding out "ghost workers" and monetization and rationalization of benefits—created some space for restructuring the recurrent budget and shifting resources to the capital budget. Particular attention was given to pro-poor expenditures within the budget, which were much needed to improve Nigeria's human-development indicators and progress toward achieving the Millennium Development Goals (MDGs).

In particular, to effectively target spending on social programs, savings from debt service (following debt relief; see chapter 6) amounting to about US$1 billion a year were channeled into specific poverty reduction programs monitored under a mechanism called the Overview of Public Expenditures in NEEDS (OPEN). As an example, in the 2006 budget, OPEN allocated funds for various MDG projects in health, education, agriculture, rural electrification, and water supply. These allocations were over and above the amounts prioritized to these sectors under the regular budget. Funds provided under the OPEN scheme have helped scale up national immunization programs, construct health-care centers, train an additional 150,000 primary-school teachers, and build small multi-purpose earth dams in virtually every state.

To address the problem of contractor and pension arrears, we instituted an audit to find out more about the nature and magnitude of the
underpayments. The audit result provided the basis to capitalize this
debt through issuance of three- to five-year bonds at competitive interest rates. For contractor arrears, the federal government issued bonds
of about 91.65 billion naira (US$715 million) between September and
December, 2006, and made cash payments of 4.6 billion naira (US$36
million) in addition. Similarly, the government addressed civil-service
pension arrears with 75 billion naira (US$586 million) in bonds and
cash payments of about 11 billion naira (US$85.6 million) (figures from
Debt Management Office and Office of the Accountant General of the
Federation). With banks willing to discount these bonds, a secondary
market was also created.

What Were the Results of the Macroeconomic Reforms?

The development of a budget framework, along with changes in the
budget process, yielded immediate and important benefits. Development priorities became clearer and better resourced. Negotiations with
the National Assembly proceeded on a sounder technical footing, even
though they did not become noticeably easier (legislators still persisted
in inflating the budget by doubling or tripling the allocations to themselves and adding their favorite "constituency" projects). Payments
of various types of government obligations were systematized and
improved. The arrears situation noticeably improved. Leakages in the
budget process did not disappear, but were considerably reduced.
Better reconciliation of accounts reduced the access to the central bank
overdraft account. The pace of implementation of the capital budget
quickened, reaching 80–90 percent. (It had been less than 50 percent
before 2004.) The cabinet also focused more on results.

The most visible result was the restoration of macroeconomic stability from 2004 to 2006. (See table A2.4.) The application of the OPFR led
to accumulation of savings in the Excess Crude Account and enabled
a less volatile revenue and expenditure path for the budget. It is indeed
remarkable to note the disappearance of volatility in government expenditures from 2003 to 2006, clearly visible in figure A2.1, and the
appearance of a visible bump between revenues and expenditures in
this period, representing savings in the Excess Crude Account. Fiscal
discipline was restored, and there was a marked improvement in the
government's consolidated fiscal balance. The previous deficit of 3.5

percent of GDP in 2003 gave way to consolidated surpluses of about 7.7 percent of GDP in 2004 and 10 percent of GDP in 2005. The increased public savings enabled Nigeria to pay off its external debt arrears of about US$6 billion and to utilize another US$6 billion in a creative debt buy-back that helped the write-off on its external debt of US$30 billion owed to the Paris Club. Foreign reserves increased from US$7.5 billion in 2003 to US$46 billion by the end of 2006.

The implementation of monetary policy was similarly disciplined, as the central bank adhered to various monetary targets and reduced inflation – from 21.8 percent in 2003 to 10 percent in 2004, though it increased slightly to 11.6 percent at the end of 2005. Similarly, interest rates, though relatively high, declined gradually. Prime lending rates declined from 21.3 percent at the end of 1999 to 17.6 percent at the end of 2005. Adoption of the Wholesale Dutch Auction System (DAS) facilitated the convergence of foreign-exchange markets and the elimination of a black-market premium.

Overall, the attainment of macroeconomic stability provided a platform for the improved growth performance seen in recent years. Growth rates averaged 8.1 percent a year from 2003 to 2006. This was a notable improvement over the decade before reform, when annual growth rates had averaged about 2.3 percent. More important, the strong growth rates have been driven by growth in the non-oil sectors of the economy, needed for job creation. Growth was especially high in agriculture, which grew at a remarkable average rate of 7 percent per year from 2003 to 2006.

With this progress, and with the debt relief obtained in 2005–06 (see chapter 6), the international financial markets began to pay attention and to see Nigeria in a more positive light. In 2006 this enabled me to invite Fitch and Standard and Poor's to give Nigeria its first-ever sovereign credit rating. Nigeria received a BB–, a rating on par with those of Brazil (the model for some of our reforms), Turkey, Venezuela, and other emerging market countries at the time. It was a true independent validation of the progress that Nigeria had made in a very short period of time. Results like these made me glad I had returned to Nigeria to tackle the challenge.

3 Promoting Privatization, Deregulation, and Liberalization

Although successful macroeconomic stabilization was necessary to restore economic growth, it was not sufficient. To get to the 7 percent per year growth rate targeted in NEEDS and sustain it, we needed to complement macroeconomic stabilization with a set of microeconomic reforms designed to change the direction and structure of the economy and lay the basis for longer-term growth. We focused on sectors and areas that our analysis showed were large drains on public finances or were blocking private-sector activity and in which economic activity tended to be marred by corruption and the role of the state was a hindrance rather than a help to economic growth.

We targeted deregulation and liberalization of the telecommunications sector, the downstream petroleum sector, and the power sector; privatization of hundreds of public-sector enterprises; reform of the civil service; reform of the trade, tariff, and customs regime; and restructuring and consolidation of the banking sector. These efforts are discussed in this chapter and the next. In some sectors we met with considerable success and unleashed economic growth; in other sectors we were less successful or achieved mixed results.

Liberalizing Important Sectors of the Economy and Privatizing Public Enterprises

Between 1973 and 1999, the Federal Government of Nigeria invested the equivalent of about US$100 billion in 590 public enterprises, 160 of them commercial, in virtually every sector of the economy, from petroleum refineries to flour mills, from telephone and electric power companies to radio stations, from oil palm plantations to car assembly plants. By the early 1980s, with oil revenues dwindling, the financial burden of maintaining these enterprises had become overwhelming.

The fiscal unsustainability of the public enterprises was an indication of broader problems. Often they were not only poorly managed but were also hotbeds of corruption, resulting in severe inefficiencies in operation and poor service delivery.

State-owned enterprises depended predominantly on financial support from the government, which came through several direct and indirect means. These included direct subventions from the budget for workers' payments, annual grants awarded for capital accumulation, discounted loans, guaranteed third-party loans to enterprises, import-duty waivers, exemptions from taxes applicable to comparable private companies, and monopoly privileges. But there were further drains on the Treasury, in the form of their very low rates of return—0.5 percent, on average)—forgone taxes on profits, mismanagement of assets, and bad debts. Between 1992 and 1999, public enterprises consumed an average US$3 billion *per year* in direct and indirect subsidies, the Bureau of Public Enterprises estimated.

Defining the Problem

Nigeria was not the only country that created state-owned enterprises. In the 1960s and the 1970s, many of the newly independent African countries did the same. In those years the view of the role of the state was vastly different. There was a much more interventionist ideology that saw the state not just as an enabler or a regulator of private enterprise but as a producer of goods and services. First, the government was seen as the primary driver of economic development, and it was expected to provide critical infrastructure and services such as power, transportation, and telecommunications at affordable prices to support economic activity in the economy. Second, given the relative weakness of the existing private sector after independence and the limited private capital available for investments, the government also participated actively in other sectors, including manufacturing, finance, and hospitality. Government spending and investment were expected to produce multiplier effects in various sectors of the economy. Third, against the backdrop of nationalism, the government wanted to encourage indigenous enterprises in the place or absence of those run by the colonial powers. Fourth, by promoting local production of goods and services, the government sought to reduce imports, in line with the prevailing import-substitution theory of the time.

The government proved to be a bad manager of businesses, however, and a poor and inefficient deliverer of basic services. Most public enterprises were persistently in a precarious financial position, generating significant debts and losses. Often unable to pay workers' salaries, they also had huge pension liabilities—more than a trillion naira (US$8.3 million) in 2003.

Moreover, the enterprises suffered from a great deal of political interference in the running of their affairs. More than 5,000 board seats were said to have been created, conferring enormous patronage powers on political leaders. Board members often saw themselves not as responsible for overseeing the organizations for the benefit of the Nigerian public, but as beneficiaries of financial payback for their political contributions. Management decisions became infected with personal and political agendas costly to the economy. Four examples of poor performance and poor service delivery illustrate this state of affairs.

Electric Power

NEPA, the Nigerian Electric Power Authority—also said in Nigeria to stand for Never Expect Power Always—was a giant public utility responsible for generating, transmitting, and distributing electricity. It consistently delivered one of the lowest levels of average per capita electricity production in the world. In 1999, when President Obasanjo took office, a review of the sector showed that no new plants had been built and no major overhauls of existing plants had taken place for a decade, that only 19 of 79 generating units were in operation, and that no transmission lines had been built since 1987. One-fourth of the average start-up cost for a business was for private power generation, and virtually all Nigerian manufacturing firms and small and medium-size enterprises had back-up generators.[1]

Telecommunications

The Nigerian Telecommunications company (NITEL), a 50-year-old government telecommunications monopoly, had been able to provide only 450,000 land lines to Nigerians by 1999, when President Obasanjo first opened the sector for licensing of new mobile providers. NITEL's mobile telephony arm, MTEL, has never been able to compete.

Oil and Gas

At the center of Nigeria's complex oil and gas sector is Nigeria's giant petroleum company, the Nigerian National Petroleum Corporation,

which controls both the upstream sector (that is, exploration and production) and the downstream sector (including four refineries that
scarcely function despite repeated investments in turn-around mainte-
nance). Because of the country's moribund refineries, very little of the
refining is done in the country; almost all the refined products are
imported. Moreover, prices of refined petroleum products were heavily
subsidized, with subsidies running close to 40 percent of the international price at the time of the reform program in 2003. A combination
of inefficiency, corruption, and unsustainable subsidies led to frequent
shortages of refined products, with long lines and rationing at gas stations nearly every day in the world's eighth-largest oil exporter. Government had to step in to bear an annual financial burden of about
US$1 billion in subsidies—out of a federal budget of around US$10
billion as of 2004—to keep petrol prices low at the pump.

Ports
The Nigerian Ports Authority, responsible for the operation of the country's seven ports, was also extremely inefficient. Thousands of tons of
imported goods slated for manufacturers were held up at the ports,
resulting in higher costs for the businesses. Nigerian port charges were
high even by West African standards. In addition, Nigerian ports were
grossly overmanned. Corruption was endemic in the ports, organized
crime was rife, and security was lax.

In addition, the Nigerian Railway Corporation, the Nigerian Gas
Company, and dozens of commercially oriented enterprises were all
operating inefficiently, running up debts, and incurring losses that
were contingent or direct liabilities on the budget. (See table A3.1.)
    The scale of the inefficiencies, the staggering financial losses, and
the poor or nonexistent service delivery to the Nigerian public and the
Nigerian economy meant that Nigerians were paying twice over for
these public enterprises. A solution was needed.

**Solving the Problem: Privatizing and Commercializing Public
Enterprises, and Deregulating and Liberalizing Important Sectors**

A search for solutions to the problem of public enterprises began well
before our efforts on reform. Successive Nigerian governments had
recognized the problem and commissioned numerous studies, starting
as far back as 1969 (the Adebo Commission) and continuing in 1973

(the Udoji Commission), in 1981 (the Onosode Commission), and in 1984 (the Al-Hakim Commission). All the studies came to the same conclusion: that the public enterprises were inefficient, corrupt, and a burden on the Treasury, and radical measures were needed to deal with them. The result was the promulgation of Privatisation and Commercialisation Decree No. 25 in 1988, and subsequently Act No. 28 of 1999. These provided the basis for a radically different approach to the public enterprises.

Despite the consensus on the need for action, privatization got off to a slow start, not least because of emotional and political issues related to the sale of national assets.[2] In 1986–87, some agricultural commodity boards and several units of the Nigerian Livestock Production Company were liquidated. In August of 1989, a Technical Committee on Privatisation and Commercialization was created to facilitate the privatization process. A total of 111 enterprises were slated for · privatization, but only 55 had been sold by 1993. The privatization program was suspended during the Abacha administration (from 1994 to early 1999).

In 1999, the democratically elected government of President Obasanjo relaunched and reinvigorated the privatization and commercialization program, including the modification of Decree 25 on privatization and its enactment as the Privatisation Act. In a July 1999 speech at the inauguration of the National Council on Privatisation, Obasanjo accused public enterprises of "gross incompetence and mismanagement, blatant corruption, and crippling complacency." The Bureau of Public Enterprises, under the leadership of Mallam Nasir El Rufai and later (2005–2007) Irene Chigbue, was strengthened, and a methodology and an institutional framework were put in place to guide the privatization, commercialization, and liberalization programs. As prominent members of the Economic Team, and with the support of team members, El Rufai and Chigbue fought many battles to keep this important part of the NEEDS agenda moving.

Methodology and Institutions for Privatization

The Privatisation Act provides the institutional and legal framework for privatization in Nigeria. It established the National Council on Privatisation to develop privatization policy and the Bureau for Public Enterprises as an implementing agency. The NCP is the chief body for making decisions on matters such as what sectors should be liberalized, which public enterprises should be privatized or commercialized, what processes should be followed, what kind of legal and regulatory framework should be established, and what remedies should be implemented to mitigate the social and economic effects of privatization, commercialization, or liberalization on citizens. It was chaired by the vice president (Atiku Abubakar chaired it during the period of the reform program), with the Minister of Finance (me) as vice chair and with Nigeria's economic decision makers as members, including the governor of the central bank, the economic adviser to the president and deputy chair of the National Planning Commission, the Minister of Justice and the Attorney General of the Federation, the secretary to the Federal Government, the Director General of the Bureau of Public Enterprises, and representatives of the labor unions and of the organized private sector. Sectoral ministers were regularly invited to meetings relevant to their sectors.

The Bureau of Public Enterprises is the implementation arm and secretariat of the National Council on Privatisation. It executes the policies determined by the NCP and provides advice and recommendations to that body on what enterprises should be privatized or commercialized and by what method that should be done. The Bureau of Public Enterprises does all the technical work, engaging advisers and consultants to assist. It prepares approved enterprises for privatization, does due diligence on interested investors, and negotiates agreements. It oversees the sale of shares of enterprises undergoing privatization, and monitors performance after privatization. It prepares enterprises for commercialization, and prepares sector policy, legal, and regulatory frameworks and bills guiding liberalization of relevant sectors for enactment by the National Assembly.

With assistance from the World Bank and the UK's Department for International Development, and with the aim of maximizing transparency, the Bureau of Public Enterprises developed a number of methods congruent with international norms for privatization and got them included in the Privatisation Act.

Transfer to Core Investor Substantial equity stake and management control is transferred to a core investor or group of investors judged by the Bureau of Public Enterprises to have the requisite technical expertise, managerial experience, and financial capacity to effectively manage the company. This option is typically selected for enterprises with good financial prospects.

Public Offer To ensure broad participation and foster a national sense of ownership, a percentage of the shares are reserved for the general public. These shares are typically presented in an initial public offering in the stock exchange, often after transfer of a company to a core investor. Companies already listed on the stock exchange are privatized by selling the governments shares to the public. The act provides that not less than 1 percent of the shares to be offered for sale to Nigerians be reserved for employees of the public enterprises being privatized.

Concessioning Instead of selling a company outright, the government may decide to lease or "concession" the company to private operators for a specified period, typically ranging from 10 to 25 years. The private investor pays an agreed-upon up-front fee to the government and is required to invest capital in the business during the period of the concession. Ports, railways, stadiums, and national parks were among the public enterprises that were concessioned.

Asset Sales and Liquidation In some cases, a company may be broken up into various assets, which are then sold individually after the company as a whole is dissolved or liquidated. This method was usually used for companies with very poor performance prospects for which it would be difficult to attract bids or interest from investors.

Commercialization There may be enterprises that the government decides to retain as owner either because they have certain public-goods characteristics or for security or other reasons. In such a case, if possible, the decision is made to commercialize the enterprise fully or partially. Such enterprises are typically restructured to make them operationally more efficient. Under full commercialization, they are expected to cover their operating and capital expenses and to make a profit. Under partial commercialization, enterprises are expected to cover operating expenses. Government-owned radio and television stations were partially commercialized. Under the Petroleum Industry Bill—a new bill that proposes to restructure the oil and gas sector—the

Nigerian National Petroleum Corporation and its subsidiaries would be fully commercialized in the manner of similar organizations in Malaysia (Petronas) and Brazil (Petrobras).

Other Methods Other methods include management/employee buyouts, private placements, willing buyer–willing seller arrangements, debt equity swaps, and public auctions.

Whatever the modalities used for privatization, the Bureau for Public Enterprises made clear that the aim was to ensure an open and transparent process for all transactions involving various stages of due process, including advertisement for advisers and core investors, due diligence on bidders, due diligence by bidders, evaluation of technical bids, and public opening of financial bids with live media coverage.

In sectors with monopoly or near-monopoly markets (such as large utilities where there are increasing returns to scale), it was important to reform and restructure the entire sector and to introduce regulations to attract private investors while protecting consumers. Typically, we began this process with the formulation (or revision) of a sector policy, which was then debated with stakeholders and revised on the basis of their input. We worked on new laws and regulations encouraging demonopolization and competition, such as the establishment of an independent sector regulator (which would be responsible for ensuring fair play and protecting the interests of consumers), licensing rules, and social obligations to the poor and to rural areas. This work also included developing and enacting a tariff regime.

Once we had these building blocks in place, the sector would be restructured and liberalized, removing the public enterprise's monopoly and opening the sector up for competition. The Bureau of Public Enterprises would then implement the privatization of affected public enterprises using one or more of the methods and processes described above.

Between 2003 and 2007, we made a particularly strong push to open up monopoly sectors to competition and sell off loss-making enterprises to the private sector, with considerable success. Despite forces arrayed against the liberalization and privatization process, we were able to show Nigerians that it was indeed possible to transform service delivery in certain sectors of the economy and to bring the country into the modern age.

Telecommunications

The biggest and most successful push happened in the telecommunications sector. Decree 75 of 1992 liberalized that sector and opened it up to competition. The National Communications Commission (NCC) was established as the regulatory authority, and the national telephone company NITEL was commercialized. A number of private companies received licenses, but not much happened to transform the sector until 2001, when the NCC auctioned three digital mobile licenses to operators Econet (now Zain), MTN, and MTEL.

The use of mobile telephony in Nigeria began to explode. In 1999, NITEL had an installed capacity of 450,000 telephone lines in the entire country. By 2007, owing to the mobile network, this number had increased to 38 million, making Nigeria the country with the world's fastest-growing teledensity. By April 2010, the number of mobile phone lines had increased to 85 million, with many people subscribing to multiple lines. The transformation of the telecommunications sector was a huge success.

This explosion was enhanced by the Telecommunications Act of 2003, which strengthened the role of the NCC and encouraged still more entry and competition in the sector. New national companies (including Glo, a Nigerian-owned mobile operator) also came on the scene. The NCC estimates that there were new investments of about US$37.5 billion in the years 2003–2007, creating about 100,000 direct jobs and about 5 million indirect jobs. The sector continues to be one of the most profitable for investors in Nigeria, while opening up hitherto unavailable services to Nigerians everywhere but especially in the rural areas. Mobile phones improved access to market information for farmers and traders, facilitated banking transactions, and improved connectivity among communities and families in both rural and urban areas and with the expansive Nigerian diaspora. Experts believe that there is still a potential for expansion, and many applications are still to be exploited. This will be enhanced by bringing the relatively high unit costs of services down, and by improving quality.

While the liberalization and deregulation of the sector was very successful, the privatization of NITEL and its mobile arm MTEL did not achieve the same success, and at various times met with widespread public criticism and controversy. There were four attempts to privatize NITEL. The first attempt (in 2001) failed because the winning bidder, Investors International London Limited, a joint

Nigerian foreign venture, famously failed to pay the balance of 90 percent of its bid price of US$1.3 billion, and the transaction was accordingly terminated.

NITEL was put under management contract for two years with the idea that perhaps it could be restructured and its operations improved, rendering it even more attractive for privatization. The contract managers (Pentascope, a Dutch-Nigerian consortium) could not pull this off and came under public criticism for failure to do so while collecting significant management fees. Its contract was terminated.

In December 2005, a second attempt was made to privatize NITEL. That attempt failed because the amount offered by the top bidder, Orascom, a well-known Egyptian-based telecommunications company, at US$256.5 million, was felt to be unacceptably low and likely to lead to public criticism of selling off "one of the country's crown jewels" at a giveaway price. In the meantime, NITEL's operations had deteriorated, the company was in decline, and its 8,000 workers were a significant burden on the public purse.

In 2006, a third attempt was made to privatize the company. Through a negotiated "willing buyer–willing seller" approach, NITEL was sold to Transcorp, a new Nigerian conglomerate put together by a group of wealthy Nigerian investors and government officials. Transcorp paid US$500 million for 51 percent of NITEL's shares, with the remaining 49 percent held by the Federal Government.

Even this sale at a more favorable price did not escape controversy. Nigerians were suspicious and very critical of a sale that looked like an inside deal to a group of the elite. An editorial in the July 9, 2006 issue of the newspaper *ThisDay* captured the public mood: "From the stalled attempt by the Investors International (London Ltd. IILL) to acquire the company, to Pentascope's controversial management of it, the NITEL story had been a running sore. After years of poor management and loss of revenue, it ought to be something of good news that the telecommunication company is now privatized. Ironically, however, that joy is being clouded by doubts. And much of this doubt stems from the controversy over the ownership and vision of Transcorp."

Even after two years, Transcorp failed to turn the fortunes of NITEL around. Consequently, in an emergency meeting on June 1, 2009, the National Council on Privatisation approved the revocation of NITEL's sale to Transcorp, citing its failure to adhere to the terms of the Share Sales Purchase Agreement and its failure to pay the salaries of staff members for more than 12 months.

A fourth and final attempt at NITEL's privatization, which commenced in 2009, was terminated in 2011 as New Generation Communications Limited and Omen International Limited—respectively the preferred and the reserve bidder—failed to pay their respective bid sums of US$2.5 billion and US$985 million.

The Ports Sector

The success in the telecommunications sector was partially replicated in the ports sector, where the 2005 Ports and Harbors Bill provided the legal anchor for the concessioning of 28 terminals in the nation's ports. The Nigerian Ports Authority served as landlord and interim regulator.

I chaired a presidential task force specially set up to deal with thorny issues of large labor redundancies and a US$595 million hole in the pension fund. Initially, negotiations with the Maritime Workers Union and others representing the staff of the Nigerian Ports Authority, as well as casual laborers, were tense. Amid an atmosphere of general lack of trust on both sides, the unions sponsored many newspaper articles and advertisements against me and against the presidential task force, accusing us of planning to throw people out of jobs in a jobless economy. Emotions ran high in negotiations, and it took many rounds to establish a measure of trust and some buy-in of the deep financial hole the Nigerian Ports Authority had created in the face of a potentially lucrative business.

We eventually came to an understanding on a reasonable package of benefits for both NPA workers and casual laborers to be made redundant, and the workforce was to be cut by more than 60 percent. The benefits would be paid for partly by selling off some of NPA's valuable property and other assets, and the remainder would be funded through the budget. Payments of about US$100 million per year in fees and royalties to government were expected, and a March 2007 monitoring report by the Bureau of Public Enterprises noted that the terminals were functioning better. By June 2006, when I became Minister of Foreign Affairs, there was still a lot of unfinished business with port reform: strengthening the regulator and sorting out regulatory functions, streamlining the number of agencies at the port, and completing ongoing port investment programs. But there was no doubt that the concessioning of terminals had recorded some success.

Reforms that we carried out in two other sectors to prepare for commercialization and privatization are also noteworthy.

The Petroleum Sector

Because Nigeria suffered from a constant and shameful shortage of refined petroleum products, we recognized that a major stumbling block to the entry of new refineries and privatization of existing ones was the existence of a price subsidy at the pump. Unless the government was prepared to phase this subsidy out and allow the market price to prevail, no private operator would have the right incentives to enter the market for refined products. The alternative was for government to continue bearing the cost of subsidies, but, as has already been noted, the burden on the budget was substantial, particularly in light of the poor targeting of this subsidy. Although poor and working-class people would feel the impact of a removal of subsidies through higher transportation costs, those benefiting most from lower prices for petroleum products were not the poor and vulnerable of the country but the car-owning middle and upper classes. Neighboring countries, including Benin, Cameroon, Niger, and Togo, were also major beneficiaries. Nigerian gasoline was plentiful in those countries, where it fetched higher prices. An illicit trade with strong vested interests had emerged around the gasoline subsidy.

In July, August, and September of 2004, when we were preparing the 2005 budget, we recommended to the president that we completely phase out the gasoline subsidy by moving the price at the pump from 34 naira to 48 naira per liter, the import parity or market price. This would save the cost of the subsidy—the equivalent of about US$1 billion—for use in the budget after redirecting some of the savings to an urban mass transport program to reduce the impact of the subsidy's removal on the poor.

Phasing out the subsidy would be a decision of enormous political sensitivity, requiring serious backing from the president. Past attempts to phase out petroleum subsidies in Nigeria in conjunction with various IMF reform programs had never succeeded and had always ended up spurring violent demonstrations, sometimes resulting in some deaths. This time I was sure that, with a Nigerian Economic Team behind the recommendation, the protests would be more muted and certainly would not result in lives lost. Unfortunately, I was to be proved wrong.

Once we had made the case to the president, the preparation left the hands of the Economic Team members and entered the political realm. We were not brought into the strategy sessions on how to handle the phase-out. We heard of lots of discussion between the president's appointed political spokespeople and labor. But it seemed to be going nowhere. We had recommended a proper communications program to explain the rationale to the public and especially to the more volatile segments of society, such as university students and the labor unions. We believed that it was necessary to engage stakeholders before such a phase-out.

But no real communications program was prepared. Instead rumors of a pending increase were rife, leading to hoarding behavior and queues. We had targeted sometime in November 2004 for phasing out the subsidy. But in late October, when I was out of the country traveling, we all heard the announcement of an increase in gas prices at the pump. Demonstrations and marches on Abuja immediately ensued, led by labor and involving civil society and students. The demonstrations went on for a few days and unfortunately turned violent. The police responded with force, and six people were killed. This was one of my lowest points in the three-year reform effort. From history I had known that such a reform could not pass without protest, but I had never dreamed that it would result in loss of lives. I was depressed for days because I felt that had the subsidy phase-out been properly prepared we could have avoided the loss of lives.

Despite the difficult circumstances, the president, to his credit, remained politically committed to the subsidy phase-out and did not back down. Labor, led by Adams Oshiomole of the Nigerian Labor Congress (now a politician and governor of Edo State), continued to insist that it would not accept the higher gasoline prices and that some compromise should be found. The president responded by setting up a working group made up of government officials (including me), legislators, labor, and representatives of civil society to work out a way to handle the matter. One proposal had been for us to consider the imposition of a small consumption tax on petroleum when prices were low. This would result in an accumulation that could then be used as a cushion to hold down rapid price increases at a time of high oil prices. Ghana and other countries seemed at the time to be succeeding with such a system, but we could not get agreement on this in the working group.

A proposal that the working group did agree on was one that we had discussed in the Economic Team. This was to cross-subsidize energy consumption by the poor by charging the market price for gasoline at the pump while targeting subsidies to kerosene, the fuel of choice for cooking and lighting for the poor. We would buttress this by subsidizing the purchase of large buses for public transport in both rural and poor urban areas. States were encouraged to co-sponsor and co-finance the bus-purchase initiative in their states. In line with good economic practice, these subsisting subsidies were clearly identified in the federal budget. By pursuing this approach, we hoped to open up the sector to entry and competition by private oil refineries.

Unfortunately, the success in phasing out generalized petroleum products subsidies and replacing this with targeted kerosene subsidies for the poor lasted only one year, through 2005. By the end of that year, oil prices on the international market were climbing higher, pushing the prices of refined products even higher. The price of a liter of petrol at the pump had gone from 48 naira to 65 naira—a 35 percent increase. To push all this onto the consumer was considered politically difficult, and unfortunately subsidies crept back. Six years later, in 2011, petroleum products subsidies are still a key feature of the Nigerian economy, totaling US$13 billion a year. Of course, there have been no entries into the business of refining oil.

The Power Sector

The other notable sectoral reform was in the power sector. Power remains one of the seemingly most intractable challenges of the Nigerian economy. As has been noted, the abysmal service delivery and the inefficiency of the power monopoly NEPA were very costly to Nigerian households and businesses, both socially and economically. Such costs mean that many Nigerian companies simply cannot compete. As a result, manufacturers in many industries have closed up shop. Others are prevented from investing because the high cost of electricity is an effective barrier to entry.

Over the years, the many attempts to improve NEPA's performance never did work, and it seemed that the only way to regain efficiencies was to break up NEPA's monopoly on the power sector and open it up to competition. In 2005, with the support of agencies such as the UK's Department for International Development and the World Bank, the Bureau of Public Enterprises incorporated NEPA as the Power Holding Corporation of Nigeria (PHCN) and transferred all functions, assets, liabilities, and staff of NEPA to PHCN.

Furthermore, the Power Sector Reform Act of 2005 saw the unbundling of 17 successor companies (five in generation, eleven in distribution, and one in transmission) out of PHCN and their incorporation in preparation for privatization. The Power Sector Reform Act also promoted the development of competitive electricity markets and established the Nigeria Electricity Regulatory Commission (NERC) as the independent regulator. Putting the institutional framework for regulation and functioning of the market in place and establishing the tariff regime has taken time. Though there had already been some entry of private investors into the generation business, entry into and exit from the electricity market were expected to increase when the process for privatization of unbundled PHCN assets truly began in December of 2010. The expectation was that the added investment and technical capacity this would truly start the transformation of the Nigerian power sector, with the long-awaited attendant benefits to the Nigerian economy.

Other Transactions and Deals

In addition to the major sectoral reforms, the Bureau of Public Enterprises used techniques and methodology described above to privatize, concession, or commercialize dozens of other public enterprises, including auto assembly plants, oil palm plantations, hotels, oil service companies, and cement and sugar factories. In all, nearly 170 companies (including 28 port concessions) were sold or taken out of government hands in the period 1999–2011. More than half of the transactions were implemented during the height of the reform program, in 2005 and 2006. (See table A3.2.)

Results, Challenges, and Opportunities

The deregulation, liberalization, and privatization agenda of the reform program was ambitious, and much progress was made. The fact that reforms met with mixed results even in the relatively successful telecommunications sector is a testimony to how difficult this agenda was and still is.

Though the opening up of the telecommunications sector was a huge success, the privatization of NITEL and MTEL continues to be uncertain. Similarly, in the petroleum sector, the initial gains with phasing out subsidies, which could have opened up the downstream sector to competition, were not sustained and were soon reversed. Nevertheless, the privatization program opened the door to a new way of doing business in many sectors of the economy. It also brought receipts from the proceeds of privatization into the Treasury—about 251.4 billion naira (the equivalent of about $US2 billion) between 1999 and 2011. Another US$10 billion in annual transfers to public enterprises was

saved as a result of these reform efforts.[3] The program attracted investment from reputable international companies such as Lafarge (France),
Holciem (Spain), and Scancem (Norway); from Dangote (a domestic
cement firm), from A. P. Møller in ports, and from the Indonesian firm
Indorama in petrochemicals.

Nigeria's program of deregulation, liberalization, and privatization
remains controversial. Part of this controversy is ideological. There is
a core of intelligentsia inclined toward socialism in Nigeria—in aca-
demia, in the media, in labor unions, and elsewhere—who, despite the
obvious failures of the state in Nigeria's case, still believe in the role of
the state as producer, employer, and equalizer in society. To them, the
whole privatization agenda, far from being an attempt to get the state
out of activities it has not done well, is a neoliberal ploy being visited
on Nigeria by the West.

Part of the controversy is due to vested interests. There were and
still are many members of the political elite who depend on the privileges and handouts from state-owned enterprises to take care of their
dependents and large numbers of hangers-on. They were always going
to be opposed to the privatization agenda.

But part of the controversy is due to a suspicion among the general
public—a suspicion that has sometimes been borne out—that not all of
the privatization agenda has been carried out in an open and transparent manner. There has been political interference (leading to reversals
of some deals), there has been a lack of transparency, and there have
been hints of corruption in the implementation of some privatizations in telecommunications, petrochemicals, steel, aluminum, and
other industries. Although these occurrences taint the privatization
agenda, their adverse effects do not outweigh the positive results that
have been obtained. Policy makers should pursue the agenda to its
logical end, along the way learning lessons on what has gone right or
wrong, particularly as to transparency, and using these lessons to conclude the privatization of the remaining public enterprises and improve
the regulatory framework of those sectors now in private hands.

4   Launching Other Structural Reforms

In addition to the structural reforms revolving around privatization, deregulation, and liberalization, we undertook parallel reforms in three main areas: civil service; trade, tariffs, and customs; and banking.

Civil-service reform was needed if we were to implement our daunting development program for the country. Preserving the government bureaucracy had become the main purpose of the budget, rather than investing in infrastructure and improved service delivery for the population. That had to change.

We also needed to tackle economic inefficiencies and corruption surrounding trade, tariffs, and customs. Failure to do so would mean that businesses might still be unable to expand and create jobs because of bottlenecks linked to customs and the trade regime.

In addition, we took steps to reform the banking sector, to bring it back to health, and above all to strengthen it to play its primary role of financing the real sector and supporting economic development.

These reforms met with varying degrees of success and pushback.

Reforming the Civil Service

A fundamental challenge that the Economic Team was asked to take on was that of reforming the federal civil service. The civil service that we met was oversized, poorly skilled, and poorly remunerated. The result was abysmally poor delivery of services to the public. Getting any kind of service—for example, getting police protection, finding out how to pay your taxes, being paid for contracts executed for government, or getting a passport or any official papers—often entailed making small and large payments to the civil servants supposed to render the service up and down the line.

At independence, Nigeria had inherited and subsequently developed one of the best and most meritocratic civil services in Africa. It was so well regarded on the continent that Nigerian senior civil servants were often requested by other African countries to help them develop and set up their own civil services or government departments. In the 1960s and the 1970s it was quite common to find Nigerian judges, teachers, and top civil servants assisting in various countries.

But during decades of military rule, the civil service was severely undermined. Public service recruitment exercises were often used as political tools to appease various constituencies. The result was a large and underskilled work force in which employees often did not possess the technical skills needed for the job. Hierarchy and seniority were often rewarded over merit or performance. Meritocracy was further undermined in 1979 by the introduction of the Federal Character Principle, which sets a quota for the number of public servants to be appointed from each state. It applies both to recruitment into the public service and to appointments to the top echelons of the service, such as permanent secretaries, directors generals, and heads of extra-ministerial departments and agencies. All six of Nigeria's geopolitical zones—south-south, southwest, southeast, northwest, northeast, and north central—must be adequately represented. Although the underlying principle is sound in a diverse country such as Nigeria, its application is said by civil servants themselves to be grossly abused, with merit often sacrificed to mediocrity as patently less qualified people get appointed to posts in the name of fulfilling the principle.

The skills gap in the civil service was important. To my consternation, I found out after an internal census of the Ministry of Finance that I ordered as part of the reform process that the bulk of my ministry staff—70 percent—were lower-level administrative staff, clerks, and cleaners with only high school education or the equivalent. Only 13 percent were graduates of universities or other tertiary institutions, and just 8 percent had degrees related to accounting or economics. Overall, the government estimated that about 70 percent of federal civil servants had no more than a high school diploma, with less than 5 percent possessing modern computer skills. Clearly such a workforce was not equipped to deliver our ambitious development program.

No one quite knew the exact size of the civil service at federal or state levels. At the time of the reform, in 2004, estimates for the core federal civil service ranged from 141,440 from the Federal Civil Service Commission to 160,000 from the Office of the Head of the Civil Service.

If extra ministerial government departments and state enterprises were added, then these estimates rose to about 1 million. Adding the states brought the number up to an estimated 2.3 million public servants.

The lack of a comprehensive census, and the poor personnel and payroll control systems, led to the phenomenon of "ghost workers"—a nefarious way for some unscrupulous civil servants to augment their incomes by adding the names of nonexistent staff to the payroll and collecting their paychecks. There were even ghost pensioners.

The remuneration structure for civil servants was a problem. Basic salaries were fairly low, and there was a complicated system of fringe benefits and perks that was vulnerable to abuse and therefore costly for the Treasury. The top civil servant, a permanent secretary, earned about the equivalent of US$1,000 a month in 2004, and a director at the next level earned about US$700 a month. But fringe benefits included official residences and cars, including operating and mainte-nance costs, domestic servants, and free official and non-official phone calls in the office and at home. This system of fringe benefits cascaded through the system from top to bottom, with those at the top benefiting the most.

Political appointees and the legislature also benefited from this system. As a minister, I was entitled to and received an official resi-dence, a car, and all of the perks listed above (though I did not make use of all of them). Given the low basic salaries, many of the fringe benefits meant for official use were thoroughly abused for personal purposes. Official cars were routinely used for unofficial business. Costly personal international calls were made at government expense from both the office and at home. The costs of refurbishing official resi-dences were routinely inflated. Government picked up the tab for virtually everything in the residences of government workers. I still remember my surprise and horror when, as Minister of Finance, I found that we had a storeroom in the ministry stocked with household goods—tea sets, electric fans, refrigerators, televisions, sugar, milk—all destined for distribution on a regular basis to government workers as fringe benefits. Staff depended heavily on fringe benefits and their abuse to live well.

Abuse had become systemic and a heavy burden for the public purse. Incentives were distorted and the abuses led to low morale among staff. There were few checks and balances. The cost to the Treasury was unsustainable as recurrent costs—wages, salaries, and operating costs, including these fringe benefits—increasingly ate up the budget, making up as much as 60–65 percent of the federal budget and therefore leaving less and less room for capital expenditure. Moreover, government ministries often refused to pay bills racked up by their civil servants, causing a severe problem of cross-debts within the system. Many ministries owed huge sums to the government telecommunications agency, to NITEL, and to the Nigerian Electric Power Authority, which in turn hindered the operation of these agencies.

The Central Role of Civil-Service Reform

In launching our civil-service reforms, we went back to first principles. We knew that an effective, efficient, accountable, and transparent public service is generally recognized by students of public administration as central to good governance. Though a good public service is not sufficient to produce good governance, a bad public service is certain to produce bad governance, even if the right accountability and other mechanisms are in place (Schiavo-Campo and Sundaram 2001). A good public service enhances governance through good public service delivery, enhanced economic policy, effective public expenditure and revenue management, fiscal sustainability, and institutional development (ibid.).

President Obasanjo recognized very early in his first administration that the civil service he was dealing with was broken and could not assist him with good or effective governance in any of the ways identified above. He expressed some frustration in a 1999 speech on civil-service reform: "The world has witnessed a lot of changes since 1979 when I left office as Head of State. Rather than being a source of innovation or productivity, our civil service has been turned to a haven for primitive accumulation and recycling of outdated ideas. One gets the impression that there is excessive bureaucratization or complication of simple procedures to inflict frustration, pain and grinding poverty on the people. The Civil Service needs to inspire hope, engender creativity, to serve as a model institution for the contemporary period. . . . Reform is imperative."

President Obasanjo initiated reforms, most of them centered on building capacity and on retraining of the top echelons of the service. There was a lot of turnover at the top, as about 40 percent of the permanent secretaries inherited from the previous administration were fired and new ones appointed. Obasanjo also ordered audits of the service and needs assessments. Audits revealed many of the problems highlighted above.

Civil-service reform during the first Obasanjo administration relied heavily on civil servants themselves, through the Office of the Head of the Service, for reform. How much buy-in the sweeping reforms would require was not clear, and the pace was slow. The 1999 reforms were not the first for the civil service. Over the years, there had been numerous commissions also designed to transform and re-professionalize the service. Some of them, including the Dotun Phillips Commission of 1988 and the Ayida Panel of 1995, had been led by highly regarded Nigerians. But either the reforms had been implemented only partially or else there was little buy-in by the civil servants, so the desired transformations never took place.

When the Economic Team took up civil-service reform as one of the key areas of focus under the National Economic Empowerment and Development Strategy, it was with the intention of modernizing and reenergizing a civil service that could support and help sustain the governance of the NEEDS reform agenda. The task looked daunting. Not only had civil-service reform not succeeded previously in Nigeria, but there were very few examples of successful public service reform programs elsewhere in the world. In addition, when reform was discussed in cabinet, there were many skeptics among colleagues. Senior civil servants harbored an even deeper degree of skepticism and suspicion of the motives of the Economic Team.

One unresolved issue was the reform process still ongoing through the Office of the Head of the Civil Service. Given this context, the Economic Team decided to approach the task differently. We agreed, as we had done with other reforms, that one of us should take the lead. Nasir El Rufai accepted that difficult task. We also felt that, given the challenges of such reform, we should not move on all fronts in all ministries at the same time. A more sensible approach would be to focus on implementing certain critical reforms in a few pilot ministries, preferably those led by members of the reform team or like-minded cabinet colleagues. Initially we identified five pilot ministries, departments, and agencies (MDAs): the Ministry of the Federal Capital Territory, the Ministry of Finance, the Ministry of Information and Communication, the National Planning Commission, and the Office of the Presidency. This list was later extended to seven pilot MDAs, and then to nine.

In addition, we turned to donors and international partners, such as the World Bank, the UK Department for International Development, and the Commonwealth Secretariat for help in creating an agency that would support implementation of the reforms. Donors were already involved in helping the Office of the Head of Service (OHS), but most felt that the pace of reform was too slow.

In 2004, the president approved the creation of a Bureau for Public Service Reform (BPSR). To head it we found a top civil servant and a dedicated believer in reform, Dr. Goke Adegoroye. The creation of the BPSR was problematic and filled with intrigue. The Economic Team tried and felt it eventually succeeded in getting the BPSR approved as an agency independent from the civil service. That way, top-flight people could be hired to staff it and it would not be suffocated or slowed down by the usual "civil service mentality." But the agency was not underpinned by any legislation or act of the National Assembly, and thus its legitimacy was sometimes questioned by the civil service bureaucracy. At the same time, the Head of Service clearly felt his authority was being undermined by the creation of a new agency to support civil-service reform, and he repeatedly said BPSR was part of his office. At a point in the reform process, conflicting versions of the BPSR's organizational diagram were floating around showing it variously as independent or as part of the OHCS, and all purportedly approved by the president.

Measures to Reform the Civil Service

With the Bureau for Public Service Reform in place and with support from various donors, we focused on four sets of critical though not exhaustive reforms.

Management of Human Resources These efforts centered around staff censuses and staffing reviews in pilot ministries, promoting and recruiting new and competent blood, removing or retiring nonperformers (including "ghost workers"), retraining staff to assist with new occupations, and introducing an Integrated Personnel and Payroll Information Management System to improve the effectiveness and efficiency in the storage of personnel records and administration of monthly payroll in such a way as to enhance confidence in staff compensation, costs, and budgeting.

Revamping MDA Operations and Systems This involved restructuring and reorganizing ministry and agency departments and their operations, including introducing information and communication technology (ICT) systems and training.

Strengthening Service Delivery This effort focused on developing vision and mission statements for ministries and the creation by the president of special units in ministries, departments, and agencies to instill a service orientation in the delivery of public services. These units, known as Servicom, were overseen by a Servicom unit in the Office of the President designed to provide monitoring and oversight to the service delivery effort. The Servicom units were created as something of an add-on to the reform efforts under way by the Economic Team. Integrating them into the overall reform effort proved a challenge.

Lessening the Fiscal Burden of the Civil Service This involved a major effort to monetize fringe benefits. The monetization policy was and remains very controversial, but the truth is that the major work on this predated reforms under the Economic Team. A presidential task force led by Chief Ufot Ekaette (then Secretary to the Federal Government) had carried out much of the preliminary work on a proper monetization framework. This work was amplified and recommendations implemented as part of the reform measures. Essentially, implementation involved quantifying and converting legitimate benefits (such as those for housing and transportation) into reasonable levels of allowances to be added on to salaries and wages at different civil service grades.

A big effort was focused on selling the existing fleets of government vehicles and housing to those government officials who were currently occupying or using them, if they wished and could afford to buy. This was done in a very transparent manner, and thereafter no new government vehicles could be purchased for individual official use. Existing vehicles were valued at market rates and sold off. Drivers previously chauffeuring these vehicles were mostly laid off, including my own driver, whom I rehired on a private basis to drive the previously official vehicle, which I purchased.

Civil servants living in government housing could purchase their residence at replacement cost rather than at the competitive open market price, in recognition of their modest salaries. For political appointees such as ministers, a minimum price was set for each house, and houses were then auctioned (sometimes live on television) to the general public. If occupants could match the highest bid on their house, they were given first option to purchase. If they could not, the house was sold off to the highest public bidder. The Federal Government owned about 32,000 houses in the Federal Capital Territory. In a massive undertaking by the FCT administration, 25,700 of these houses were sold, realizing about 68 billion naira, according to FCT officials.

In sum, not only were one-off revenues realized for the budget, but the continuous burden of the recurrent maintenance costs for cars and houses was lifted from the government budget. The success of the FCT auction led the president to order the sales of government housing in Lagos, the former federal capital, where the government owned a large stock of housing in choice areas. However, this latter exercise was put under the aegis of a separate committee headed by another cabinet member. The rules of the game were not made clear in this case, and there were plenty of accusations of lack of transparency, which tainted the process and gave monetization a bad name.

Other Complementary Measures
Parallel to the civil-service reforms, the president took on a number of other complementary measures.

Reviewing Civil Servant Pay Scales The president set up a commission, headed by former interim president Ernest Shonekan, to review the pay scales of civil servants. The commission initially recommended public-sector wage increases of 25 percent starting in 2007, with a further 10 percent annual increase for the next 10 years (plus cost of living adjustments). A further review of these recommendations indicated that full implementation would result in unsustainable growth of the wage component of the budget to 45 percent. The Federal Government consequently opted for a 15 percent wage increase by 2007, with further increases to be based on progress in implementation of further public service reforms. As a result of the wage adjustment and the monetization of fringe benefits, a director's remuneration, for example, went up by 80 percent, from US$700 per month to US$1,260.

Reforming the Pension Scheme Another complementary reform, not handled directly by the Economic Team but very important to the effort to reform the civil service, was reform of Nigeria's pay-as-you-go pension scheme. This scheme, noncontributory and unfunded, with liabilities supposed to be met from current revenues, was broken. In 2003, when I became Minister of Finance, the pension scheme was characterized by consistent payment defaults and huge arrears of unpaid pensions to public service pensioners, including the military. Arrears of about a trillion naira had accumulated.

One of my most disturbing experiences as Minister of Finance was reading floods of letters from pensioners or their families complaining about former government civil servants living in extreme hardship and near death or already dead because they had not received their pensions and lacked the wherewithal to take care of themselves properly. Various groups of pensioners, including retired university teachers (friends and colleagues of my parents—who were pensioners themselves, and did not receive their pensions regularly), military, and ordinary civil servants, sent delegations from their associations to complain about the lack of, or inconsistency in, the payment of their pensions. I dreaded these encounters with upstanding citizens who had given to their country but were now being let down. I also heard complaints about the pension system from current civil servants who feared that when their time came they would not have a pension system to fall back on. This affected morale and, I believe, also fed into a culture of corruption among many of the civil servants, who pilfered to take care of their old age.

It was a credit to President Obasanjo that he recognized the importance of the problem and wanted to solve it. To lead the reform he appointed Fola Adeola, a highly respected retired managing director of one of the country's most respected banks.

Borrowing from the good practices of other developing countries and emerging market countries, and particularly from Chile, Nigeria's pension system moved from a defined benefit to a defined contribution system. Private pension administrators and custodians were selected on the basis of very stringent financial and integrity criteria, and a strong regulatory framework was put in place in the form of a Pensions Commission. The hallmarks of the new system are full funding, no arrears for government, and on-time payment of pensioners, with benefits dependent on the rate of contribution and returns from management of pension assets.

In addition, Nigeria has accumulated a pool of investible savings. As of the end of 2010, Nigeria's pension system has accumulated assets of as much as 1.1 trillion naira (about US$7.5 billion)—a clear success. We also found innovative ways to deal with most of the pension arrears, for which we offered 3-year to 5-year bonds at market rates of interest. I was particularly proud of the fact that, with Bode Agusto (then Director General of the Federal Budget Office), we worked out a scheme

with the banks to facilitate a secondary market in these bonds so that
pensioners interested in cashing out early could do so at a discount.

Results, Challenges, and Opportunities
The effort to reform the civil service was incomplete, and the results
were mixed. An overall assessment would not term it a success. The
primary reason was the limited buy-in by most civil servants and ministers. The reforms did not really expand beyond the pilot ministries,
and even within those ministries there were questions about the depth
and the acceptance of the reforms. The lack of expansion at the federal
level also meant that there were virtually no efforts to reform state or
local government services.

There was the constant tension between the efforts of the Economic
Team and those of the Head of Service and his Office, though eventually there was some rapprochement. I am not sure that the Economic
Team made every effort it could have made to win over the civil servants. We tried very hard to engage at the beginning of the reforms
through various meetings and forums, but we could feel the latent
hostility and skepticism. After a while we stopped trying and forged
ahead to implement the reforms despite the civil servants. I think
they saw us as arrogant and as unsympathetic to their roles and their
importance. We saw them as intransigent, hierarchical, and resistant to
reforms. Needless to say, this did not make for good collaboration or
dialogue. Furthermore, civil servants had little incentive to maintain
momentum for the reforms once the Economic Team was gone.

Nevertheless, the efforts to reform the civil service had some success.
An Integrated Personnel and Payroll Information System was introduced to address the "ghost worker" syndrome. About 8,000 "ghost
workers" were removed from the payrolls of the ministries in which
the IPPIS was introduced. In addition, functional and other staff reviews and "rightsizing" of some ministries, departments, and agencies
led to 30,000 layoffs. This was a great achievement in the face of so
much resistance to reform. Moreover, the president approved the hiring
of 1,000 top university graduates, underscoring the need to bring in the
right skills to the civil service.

The monetization of benefits, including the sale of houses and cars,
though still controversial among public servants and politicians in
Nigeria today, can be termed a success because it has lessened the
financial burden on the public purse. The controversy is linked to the
impact on new legislators and ministers, who now must find their

own housing (though they get housing and furniture allowances to assist) and to the fact that some of the old abuses may be creeping back in the form of purchase of official vehicles under different guises and excuses.

Since the reform efforts of the Economic Team, there have been other efforts at reform, especially the renewal of the top echelons of the service (permanent secretaries, directors, and the like). These efforts were designed to make the civil service less sclerotic and more dynamic. It is not clear that all these efforts combined have made for a more effective or efficient Nigerian civil service to date, but the direction of reform has been set.

Trade, Tariff, and Customs Reforms

Reforming Nigeria's trade regime and its Customs Service turned out to be extremely difficult and perhaps the most uncertain among the reforms we pursued. Customs reform, in particular, was a failure. Nevertheless, it is important to touch on these reforms to illustrate how vested interests can completely derail or damage positive change so important to a nation's economic sustainability.

Numerous studies by the World Trade Organization, the World Bank, the International Monetary Fund, and other international organizations have shown that trade is an important determinant of growth and of improved living standards, and that trade can sometimes have a greater effect on a country's economic development than aid (see IMF 2006). A country's trade policies and its degree of openness matter. Nigeria is a fairly open economy whose trade is dominated by petroleum exports (96 percent of exports, by value) and imports of a wide range of consumer and capital goods. Many of the problems with trade were really on the import side, as cumbersome tariff regimes and inconsistent government policies made it difficult for investors to benefit as significantly as they could from the broader macroeconomic and structural changes ongoing in the economy.

For two decades before economic reform, Nigeria's trade regime was viewed as complex, restrictive, and opaque.[1] After the structural adjustment program (SAP) of 1988 (a program that both the World Bank and the IMF endorsed), a seven-year tariff schedule with significantly reduced tariff averages was adopted. However, further downward tariff revisions were made, often in response to pressures from domestic lobbies. Since 1978, the government had also introduced policies that banned the importation of selected products that either play a strategic role in the economy or are produced by "infant industries" that need protection. Ad hoc import prohibitions and tariff revisions reduced the transparency and predictability of the tariff regime, as tariffs applied at ports could differ from published tariffs. Tariff revisions could include decisions to waive tariffs completely for certain imports. This latter practice was politically charged, as influential businesspeople often tried and succeeded in getting waivers for their imports, sometimes reaping benefits of tens of millions of dollars. Before the reforms we implemented, Nigeria maintained a complex tariff structure with about 19 bands and 5,146 lines (at the HS-8 digit level), with tariffs ranging between 2.5 and 150 percent. At various points there were up to 100 import prohibitions in place.

Two incidents related to ad hoc import prohibitions and waivers illustrate the damage vested interests can do to trade and to the overall economy.

I remember vividly an early morning meeting sometime in February 2005 between President Obasanjo and some businessmen shortly after the president's family's 6:30 a.m. prayers, in which I and a handful of other close advisers were privileged to participate. These businessmen were manufacturers who had come to complain about competition from imports. One, a manufacturer of glass bottles, complained that bottlers of drinks and other manufacturers using bottles were importing bottles from abroad and ruining his business on the pretext that they could not get the quantity and specifications they needed in Nigeria. He said this was wrong, and he could produce all the bottles needed in the country. But unless the president banned imports of bottles, he could not compete and he would have to close his factory and lay off workers, adding to unemployment. This got the president upset, and he immediately said he would prohibit imports of bottles. I tried to interject to request a quick review of the issue to ascertain the facts from all sides before imposing the ban, but the president, who knew I was generally against import prohibitions (because they tend not to work and can have adverse consequences), ruled me out of order and imposed the ban. Importing bottles of all kinds was banned. This had an immediate deleterious effect on manufacturers of pharmaceuticals and cosmetics, many of whom used small and oddly shaped bottles not manufactured in Nigeria. It took six months of outcries and lobbying by this latter group, and significant loss of domestic and regional trade, before the president could be convinced that the blanket ban was doing more harm than good and needed to be better differentiated.

Another example was the prohibition on importing textiles. This was ostensibly to protect our domestic textile industry from cheap and substandard imports. It was particularly meant to protect African cotton wax cloth and hand-tied indigo cloth. African producers of cotton wax cloth were being devastated by unfair competition from China. The Nigerian intellectual property embodied in the cloth designs was being replicated in China and then sent back to Nigeria at much lower prices, thereby undercutting the local manufacturers. The president banned importation of textiles. The implementation of this edict was so broad that all types of textiles, ranging from jute bags to carpets to finished garments that were never intended for the ban, were prohibited. This devastated Nigeria's budding fashion industry because designers could not import the range of textiles needed to mix and match with Nigerian cloth. It also damaged the emerging modern retail shops business in new shopping malls, as anchor stores could not import finished garments from their bulk manufacturers. In the meantime, the prohibition of the fake African cloth did not seem to work well either. Vast quantities continued to be smuggled in, greatly undermining the profitability of the local Nigerian cotton textile wax industry.

If the impulse to prohibit imports—no matter how misguided or misapplied—had some redeeming features of trying to protect Nigerian manufactures and jobs, the granting of waivers of import tariffs seldom had such features. Regulations of the Ministry of Finance (and later provisions under the Economic Community of West African States Common External Tariff) indicated that waivers could be granted—for example, for importation of certain types of capital goods being brought in by investors (as an incentive), or for essential medicines. The Minister of Finance was authorized to grant such waivers upon full justification to and approval of the president.

In practice, the granting of waivers was opaque and much abused. It was a steady source of corruption for mid-level bureaucrats in the ministry, for top ministry officials, and for well-heeled businesspeople and their political patrons, all of whom got payoffs because of the approved waivers. It made the playing field very uneven for businesspeople: if a competitor could obtain a waiver for import of its inputs or other needed materials, it got a huge competitive advantage. Ad hoc waivers cost the Treasury billions of dollars in lost revenue over the years—as much as 23.4 billion naira (US$155 million equivalent) in 2009.

During my time as Minister of Finance, my position on waivers was very clear and was well known, as was my position on import bans. I was against waivers except in the most clearly justified of cases. I rarely sought approval for or signed a waiver, except in a handful of well-defined cases. Evidence in ministry files of the time shows that most people seeking waivers usually waited until I was out of town traveling and had delegated my powers.

In fact, it is well known that my refusal to support duty waivers for importation of rice and other products for certain very influential businesspeople and their politician patrons as a means of financing the 2007 elections contributed to my being moved from the post of Minister of Finance to that of Minister of Foreign Affairs, and thus to my subsequent resignation from the government when I felt that the principles on which I had come to serve were no longer being respected. I had been approached on a certain night in mid 2006, first by a couple of well-known politicians and later again by one of them, who said they came with backing from even higher political quarters to ask that I grant waivers for zero import tariffs on very large shipments of rice (rice was then on the 50 percent tariff band to encourage domestic production), which would be brought into the country by well-known businesspeople and sold at high prevailing domestic prices. By my calculations, if they brought in and sold the quantities being talked about, they could easily make more than US$1 billion equivalent in Nigeria's large consumer market.

I said No for two reasons. First, I felt it was simply wrong to have encouraged large numbers of farmers to invest in planting rice with the expectations of a certain market price and then allow large quantities of a superior rice variety to be imported into the country close to harvest time, at essentially subsidized prices to compete with their output. This would be unfair competition. Farmers would lose and would be discouraged from investing in rice production in the future. Second, if there was a need for campaign finance for political parties, distorting the trade regime and demoralizing farmers was simply not the best way to go about it. In addition, it created a very uneven playing field for all. My refusal to go along earned me a strong rebuke and a threat from one of the influential politicians: "Some people feel they are very important, but we shall soon show them they are not as important as all that."

I was not politically naive. I knew that campaigns had to be financed, and I suggested other less harmful, less distorting, and more transparent ways to financing them. But importing rice was so much easier and so much more murky. More people could share in the proceeds. So the politicians felt I was in the way as Minister of Finance and had to be moved so they could benefit more easily from waivers of import tariffs.

Tariff Reforms

Though we were not able to do away with waivers on import tariffs, and we did not succeed in persuading President Obasanjo to lift some of the deleterious prohibitions, we did manage to implement some reforms to the tariff regime. Beginning in 2006, we were able to persuade the president to support Nigeria's liberalization of its import-tariff regime through adoption and implementation of the Economic Community of West African States (ECOWAS) Common External Tariff. This was in keeping with the commitment of governments of the West African states to simplify their tariff structures and improve transparency and predictability of trade policies in the subregion by adopting a common set of tariffs.

This external restraint, to which Nigeria fortunately had agreed but unfortunately had not implemented, was very helpful in bringing some order to Nigeria's trade regime. Nigeria adopted a four-band arrangement with duty rates of zero (for capital goods), 5 percent (for raw materials), 10 percent (for intermediate products), and 20 percent (for finished goods). A temporary 50 percent band, permitted under the Common External Tariff to give the country some flexibility in its future industrial policies, was added, with the understanding it would be phased out by the end of 2007. For example, the 50 percent tariff was levied on goods in which the country had a comparative advantage and aimed to support domestic production, such as rice, vegetable oils, and starch. Existing import prohibitions were also to be progressively eliminated.

The adoption of the ECOWAS Common External Tariff, though not a panacea, had the benefit of bringing some order and simplification to the tariff regime. The simple unweighted average tariff rate went from 29 percent to 18 percent, and the weighted average tariff rate from 25 percent to 17 percent. But serious problems with the country's trade regime remain. The 50 percent tariff band has not been phased out as envisaged. More important, waivers and import prohibitions are still prevalent. Our reforms in this area were only the beginning of a process that still has a long way to go.

Customs Reforms

To accompany the reforms to the tariff regime and the concessioning of ports to the private sector, I felt it was very important to reform the Customs Service. Customs administers the tariff regime and carries out the trade facilitation that is a complement. The drive to reform customs also arose from the numerous and constant complaints from the business community about the Customs Service as an impediment to their business. During my three years in office as Minister of Finance, Customs was the most complained about service of the ministry. And the Customs Service, like so many such services the world over, had a reputation for corruption and inefficiency. It would be one thing to accomplish the macroeconomic reforms targeted under NEEDS, but businesses might still be unable to expand and create jobs because of bottlenecks linked to customs and the trade regime. It was therefore important to focus on the necessary changes in this service.

The Nigerian Customs Service (NCS) was established in 1891 under British colonial rule to do two things: collect revenues and excise taxes for the Treasury and conduct anti-smuggling activities to protect the country from dangerous and unwarranted imports and exports. Over the years, a third function, trade facilitation, was added, but never quite took hold as the first two functions did. Since Nigeria's independence in 1960, and in particular since 1975, the NCS has been the subject of numerous reviews by presidential task forces or committees that have made many recommendations designed to transform and modernize it, but, these recommendations have never been fully or satisfactorily implemented.

The NCS that I encountered in 2003 was far from a modern service. It had three main problems: lengthy and inefficient systems and processes compounded by a lack of modern technology, equipment, and needed infrastructure; inadequate human resources and necessary skills and incentives; and, most important, massive corruption. These problems were compounded by the inconsistency and lack of transparency in government policies described earlier in regard to trade and tariff policies. Not only were these problems costing the Treasury money in terms of lost revenues from corruption; they also were costing the economy in terms of jobs and growth. For instance, delays for clearance of cargoes were especially long. Owing to the combined inefficiency of Customs and other numerous agencies at the ports, clearance times at Nigerian ports were 14 days or more, whereas the international standard was about 48 hours.

Corruption in Customs had and still has many dimensions. There were payoffs to Customs officers (and officials of as many as thirteen other agencies at the ports) to clear cargo. There was the seizure and auctioning of illegal and overtime cargoes to cronies and friends and influential persons. Often traders would illegally import container loads of prohibited items with the hope they could somehow do an under the table deal and get them through—and often they could.

But sometimes deals did not work and the goods were seized. Sometimes importers could not or would not clear their cargoes because of inability to pay the required duty or file the proper paperwork, or simply refused to pay bribes to get the goods through. Once such goods exceeded a designated time at the ports, they were declared overtime cargoes subject to disposal. The Customs law and regulations give a lot of discretion to the NCS, especially the comptroller general, on how to dispose of seized or unwanted cargoes. Though it was accepted that auctions to the public were a good and fair practice, in reality goods were often auctioned directly to designated individuals at favorable prices, or even assigned free.

Various segments of society benefited. Containers of seized goods were either auctioned or assigned to politicians or their relatives, to government bureaucrats, to traditional rulers from all parts of the country, or to the Security Services. Customs officials themselves had access to a fair quantity of these goods. Hundreds or thousands of dollars could be made from selling off seized second-hand cars, textiles, consumer goods of all types, construction materials, and the like. The NCS, and in particular its top brass, made friends in all strata of society, and thus enjoyed an unprecedented type of protection.

There was also a great deal of corruption linked to smuggling. Huge amounts of goods were smuggled into the country under the very noses of NCS officials. Now and again there would be interdictions and goods would be seized. But most times the smuggled goods found their way into domestic markets, causing great harm to domestic manufacturers. For instance during my time in the Ministry of Finance, Nigerian tire manufacturers and Nigerian textile wax manufacturers complained bitterly about unfair competition from smuggled goods. Eventually the influx of smuggled goods contributed to many textile and tire factories closing, with the loss of more than 100,000 jobs in the case of textiles. The disturbing point was that hardly any smugglers were caught or charged with crimes. Nigeria must be one of the few countries in the world where smugglers are known and talked about openly, and where these same big-time smugglers walk around freely in the corridors of power.

President Obasanjo, like many of his predecessors, was acutely aware that the NCS was dysfunctional and maybe even broken. In his second term in 2004, he set up a task force to review and make recommendations for reform that could build on earlier reform attempts. This task force was chaired by my deputy, the Minister of State for Finance. Recommendations of this task force centered around the need to upgrade and modernize NCS systems and processes through the introduction of higher-quality software for the automation of cargo clearance procedures and collection of customs data (the migration from the standard version of the Automated System for Customs Data, AYSCUDA, to an enhanced version, AYSCUDA++), and a move from pre-shipment inspection abroad of goods destined for Nigeria to destination inspection.

Pre-shipment is a process introduced to reduce the fraudulent shipment of goods by having them inspected abroad, before departure, by licensed and globally recognized inspection agents, such as Cotecna, Societé Generale de Surveillance (SGS), and Bureau Veritas. Destination inspection allows the goods to be inspected on arrival instead, using risk-management techniques and modern technology (e.g., scanners and x-ray machines) to detect fraudulent or dangerous cargo. The task force also recommended upgrading the human resources of the NCS through training, better incentives, and improved infrastructure in terms of offices and housing, especially for those operating at the border posts.

The recommendations were strong on the "hardware" of infrastructure, equipment, and technology; they were less so on the "software" of human development and work culture. It was clear to me that a great deal of change management would be needed to truly reform customs. The culture of corruption endemic in the service would have to change. Otherwise, the new technology would either be bypassed or undermined.

For months after the completion of the task force work, no action was taken to implement the recommendations. During this hiatus, I seized the opportunity to ask the president's permission to reexamine the work of the task force, with the objective of strengthening the recommendations by infusing a change-management component that could work on the "software" of human resources training, attitudes, and culture, as well as on systems and processes that would bring greater transparency to the work of the NCS. In July of 2005, the president gave permission for the formation of yet another Presidential Task Force on Customs Reform, this time headed by me and with five members of the Economic Team (Nasir El Rufai, Obiageli Ezekwesili, Nenadi Usman, Nuhu Ribadu, and Bode Augusto) as members. The Comptroller General of Customs, J. G. Buba, was also a member, as was Comptroller Abdullahi from the Imo/Abia State customs command. The private sector was represented by the CEOs of two major Nigerian companies: Bunmi Oni (then CEO of Cadbury, Nigeria Plc) and Tony Ezenna (chairman and CEO of Orange Drugs). After a month of study and deliberations—including interactions with various stakeholders in the sector, such as licensed Customs agents (private-sector persons licensed to complete customs procedures and clear goods on behalf of importers)—we concluded that it would be necessary to contract a competent international organization skilled in implementing customs reform if we were to achieve the objectives of the previous and present presidential task forces. The idea was that such an organization would bring coherence and professionalism to the implementation of various recommendations for changes in processes and systems, installation of hardware and software, improvements in infrastructure, training of human resources, and a thoroughgoing culture change that would tackle corruption.

Research showed Crown Agents of the UK to be the world leader in such reform. We initiated a dialogue with Crown Agents to learn more about their vision, appetite, and capability for such an assignment. It is important to note that the task force was not unanimous in approving this course of action. Some members seemed to have reservations. In particular, J. G Buba, then comptroller general of Customs, did not consider it necessary to introduce consultants to assist in the process of customs reform, believing that the NCS was quite capable of implementing the changes itself with some technical assistance perhaps from the World Customs Organization. Our interactions with Crown Agents showed that they would be capable of delivering on the assignment. We asked for a request for proposal setting out how they would implement the task, what the indicators of success would be, how they could be monitored and held accountable, and what the cost would be.

After I briefed the president, he expressed support for the proposed course of action. He then suggested that the next step should be a memorandum to the Federal Executive Council, which could be discussed and approved at one of that council's weekly meetings. While discussions with Crown Agents and preparations of the council's memo were under way, articles began to appear in the press accusing me of trying to re-colonize the Customs Service by bringing back our former British colonial masters in the guise of Crown Agents. I began to get direct and indirect feedback from various quarters that the top brass of NCS were against my proposals. There were innuendos from those giving me this feedback that I could suffer adverse consequences if I did not desist from the proposed reforms. The outcry seemed orchestrated. I was told that traditional rulers, politicians, the Security Services, and even top bureaucrats at State House were all against the idea of bringing in Crown Agents. The level of hostility was high, but I remained completely defiant because it was clear to me that this was a fight to keep the last bastion of corruption going. I went again to see the president, and this time he was distinctly lukewarm about bringing the Council memo but told me I could go ahead if I wished—less than a full endorsement.

On October 25, 2005, I brought a memorandum to the Council asking for approval to implement the full range of customs reforms identified by both the first and second Obasanjo Presidential Task Forces on Customs reforms. "It is imperative to mention," the memo explicitly stated, "that the consultants Messrs Crown Agents in the pursuit of the above listed activities are not to take over the activities of the Nigerian Customs Service but to work in close collaboration with the NCS personnel with the aim of strengthening the Service." I had just completed my presentation of the memo to the cabinet when seven hands shot up and cabinet member after cabinet member took the floor to criticize the memo and say it was unworkable, an unnecessary expense for consultants, and so on.

Based on this attack on the memo, the president concluded the discussion by saying that opposition within cabinet was such that the approvals sought within the memo could not be given and the memo should be withdrawn. It was a dramatic and painful end to an important set of reforms, and the only time I presented a memo to cabinet and failed to get it through. It was no less painful when I discovered later that the attack on the memo in the cabinet meeting had been carefully planned and orchestrated. This orchestration was carried out by some of the powerful forces within government and society, whose vested interests would be damaged by a reformed Customs Service.

A few weeks later, my deputy was instructed to bring back a revised form of the memo to cabinet requesting approval for implementation of the equipment and technology changes, infrastructural developments, some human resource developments, and implementation of destination inspection. For the latter, contracts were let to three service providers: Cotecna Destination Inspection Nig Ltd; SGs Scanning Services; and Global Scan Systems Ltd. Another company, Webb Fontaine, was recruited to implement the migration from AYSCUDA to AYSCUDA ++. There was no effective link between the service providers, and not much depth or coherence to the reforms. Above all, none of the contracted companies had the mandate to undertake change management for the new systems or to fight the endemic corruption.

Some changes resulted from the limited reforms approved by the cabinet. The NCS benefited from some improvements in infrastructure. The headquarters building in Abuja was upgraded, training colleges in Ikeja and Kano were renovated, and ICT software and hardware was improved, improving connectivity between Customs and other partner agencies. Some capacity building and training of officers occurred. But, essentially, several years later, service delivery from Customs has improved only slightly and corruption remains rampant. Private-sector operators are often reluctant to speak out for fear of being victimized.

Following the recommendations of President Obasanjo's two customs-reform task forces, President Yar'Adua also inaugurated a task force before his death in office, and so did President Goodluck Jonathan in August 2010. The task of this latter Reconstituted Presidential Task Force on Customs Reforms is to build on the work of all the previous task forces to solve the same problems that confronted us during the Obasanjo administrations and during earlier regimes. This latest task force has made recommendations similar to those we made earlier but also including recommendations to revamp the 50-year-old law governing the NCS. The hope is faint that they will succeed where others failed, because the NCS is still in the grip of the same layers of vested interests that prevented its reform year after year. It will take bold and committed steps by a newly elected president supporting a strong Economic Team to make reform happen.

Reforms in the Banking Sector

Among the most important reforms carried out during this period were those in the banking sector. Those reforms were primarily led and implemented by Professor Charles Chukwuma Soludo, a member of the Economic Team who was first economic adviser to the president and later governor of the Central Bank of Nigeria (CBN).

In July of 2004, when the reforms began, Nigeria had 89 banks with 3,300 branches. Most had a capital base of less than US$10 million, and several had bad balance sheets. The banking sector was highly concentrated, with the ten largest banks accounting for about half the industry's total assets and liabilities. The remaining 79 banks were small but had heavy fixed and operating costs, resulting in very high average costs for the industry. The attempts to cover these costs led to wide spreads between deposit and lending rates, and to a focus on lucrative short-term arbitrage of foreign-exchange "round-tripping" rather than on lending to the real sectors.

Central Bank Governor Soludo put it this way in a speech to a special meeting of the Bankers Committee in Abuja on July 6, 2004: "I am sure many of you would agree with me that some of our banks are not engaged in strict banking business in terms of savings intermediation—they are traders—trading in foreign exchange, in government treasury bills, and sometimes in direct importation of goods through phony companies. This is not healthy for our economy." He went on to summarize the major problems of Nigerian banks: weak corporate governance, as evidenced by high turnover in the Board and management staff, inaccurate reporting, noncompliance with regulatory requirements, questionable ethics, and adversarial marketing of other banks in the industry; late publication or nonpublication of annual accounts, which reduces the effectiveness of market discipline in ensuring banking soundness; gross insider abuses, resulting in huge nonperforming insider-related credits; insolvency, as evidenced by negative capital adequacy ratios and shareholder funds that had been completely eroded by operating losses; weak capital bases, even for those banks that have met the minimum capital requirement, which currently stands at 1.0 billion naira, or US$7.53 million, for existing banks, and 2.0 billion naira, or US$15.06 million, for new banks; overdependence on public-sector deposits; and neglect of small and medium-size savers. Governor Soludo proposed a set of reforms that would strengthen and consolidate the Nigerian banking sector, making it strong nationally

Box 4.1
Proposed Banking Reforms

Governor Soludo proposed thirteen major reforms in 2004:

• an increase in the minimum capital base of banks from 2 billion to 25 billion naira, with a deadline of December 31, 2005 for full compliance
• phased withdrawal of public-sector funds from banks
• consolidation of banks through mergers and acquisitions
• adoption of a risk-focused and rule-based regulatory framework
• adoption of zero tolerance in the regulatory framework, especially in the area of data and information rendition and reporting
• automation of the rendition process of returns by banks and other financial institutions through the electronic Financial Analysis and Surveillance System
• establishment of a hotline and a confidential Internet address for all Nigerians wishing to share any confidential information with the governor of the Central Bank of Nigeria
• strict enforcement of the contingency planning framework for systemic banking distress
• establishment of an Asset Management Company as an important element of distress resolution
• promotion of the enforcement of dormant laws, especially those relating to the issuance of bad checks and the law relating to the vicarious liability of the boards of banks in the case of bank failure
• revision and updating of relevant laws and drafting of new ones relating to effective operations of the banking system
• closer collaboration with the Economic and Financial Crimes Commission in the establishment of the Financial Intelligence Unit and the enforcement of the anti-money laundering and other economic crime measures
• rehabilitation and effective management of the mint

but also setting it up as a regional and global player. The main elements of the reform are summarized in box 4.1.

The announcement of the reforms, but particularly the significant upward revision of the minimum capitalization requirements and the consolidation through mergers and acquisitions, sent shock waves through the financial sector at large and the banking industry in particular. Even the Economic Team was taken by surprise. Although we had an idea that some important changes were going to be put in place for the banking sector and we were all agreed that action was needed, the details were not discussed with or known to members of the team before the announcement. Some of us on the team felt the reform proposals could have benefited from more discussion, including the possibility of allowing for niche or specialized banks to complement the universal banking model that was emerging. Nevertheless, we also understood the need for a certain degree of surprise in the undertaking to prevent vested interests from torpedoing the reforms.

Although the idea of consolidation was eventually embraced by most sections of the banking community (those who could see the opportunities in it), others were not so happy, especially about the limited amount of consultation and the fact that they might have to give up family-owned banks in the process of consolidation. Governor Soludo confirmed several unpleasant incidents, including threats to his life, during the implementation process.

Results of Reforms in the Banking Sector

How successful were the reforms, and how effective were they in transforming the Nigerian banking industry? At the end of the 18-month implementation period (December 2005) decreed by the CBN, most observers of the Nigerian financial sector judged the reforms largely successful.

Through mergers and acquisitions, the number of banks had been reduced from 89 to 25, and their capital base had been raised from 2 billion naira (US$15 million) to 25 billion naira (US$192 million) or more. Second, in the process of meeting the new capital requirements, banks raised the equivalent of about US$3 billion from the local capital market in initial public offerings, thus deepening the capital market, and attracted about US$652 million of foreign direct investment into the Nigerian banking sector. Third, a period of explosive growth followed the consolidation. Between June 2006 and June 2008, the number of bank branches grew by 54 percent, the number of deposit accounts by 39 percent, and total loans and advances by 197 percent. Fourth, bank credit to the private sector grew by 60 percent in 2007 and another 90 percent in 2008, as evidenced by the growing wedge between total assets and deposits in 2006 and 2007. Fifth, credit to the private sector financed large infrastructure projects and oil and gas projects. Agriculture and small and medium-size enterprises did not benefit much from this expansion. Credit also went into so-called margin lending to buy stocks. This would lead to problems when the 2008 global financial crisis hit. Sixth, Nigerian banks have become regional players, opening branches or buying into existing banks in most West African countries and making incursions into eastern Africa. Several have also opened offices abroad, especially in the UK.

We complemented the CBN's banking consolidation reforms with a similar approach in the insurance industry. Reform of this sector was similarly meant to strengthen insurance's contribution to the real economy. The industry was fragmented, with 103 relatively small businesses unable to take on insurance required for oil and gas, heavy infrastructure, and other sectors, with the result that most of this business went offshore. The reform aimed to consolidate the sector to about 30 businesses with a capitalization of about US$1.6 billion. To implement this, the Ministry of Finance, together with the insurance industry regulator, the National Insurance Commission (NAICOM), revised upward the required minimum paid up capital for the various categories of the insurance business. As an example, life insurance businesses were required to increase capital to about US$15 million from about US$1.2 million, while general insurance businesses had to raise their capital base to US$23 million from US$1.5 million.

Emerging Problems in the Financial Sector and the Impact of the Global Financial Crisis

The positive developments in the financial sector were curtailed by the emergence of problems in the banking sector, which in turn were worsened by the onset of the global financial and economic crisis in 2008–09. It had always been clear that the key to sustainable development of the banking sector would be a strong regulatory and risk-management regime, to be implemented by the CBN as the main regulator. As the sector's explosive growth continued, it became increasingly clear that weak regulation and supervision were problems. Senior figures at the CBN seemed caught in the optimism and excessive exuberance of the period and did not push for the strong supervisory and regulatory oversight needed, despite the strong rhetoric during the reforms.

In addition, as capital surged into the banks, it appeared that major aspects of the 2004 reforms had not worked well. There were serious failures of corporate governance at the banks and insufficient disclosure and transparency about banks' financial positions. There were significant flows into the stock market in the form of margin loans and proprietary trading disguised as loans. As Sanusi Lamido Sanusi (Professor Soludo's successor as governor of the CBN) noted in a speech he gave on February 26, 2010, the excess liquidity flowing into the stock market led to an increase in the market capitalization of the Nigerian Stock Exchange by a factor as great as 5.3 between 2004 ánd its peak in 2007. During the same period, the capitalization of bank stocks increased by a factor as great as 9. The surge of liquidity into the stock market led to steep increases in prices, and then to an asset bubble.

It is worth elaborating on the weak corporate governance that contributed to, and exacerbated, the exuberance witnessed in the banking sector and the capital markets. The development of capacity and the sophistication of bank boards had not kept pace with the complexity of the larger consolidated banks. The boards of some banks were not independent and were unduly influenced by the personality and strength of the leadership of their institutions. Insider trading and outright corruption of bank CEOs and board members, prevalent before consolidation and supposedly swept away by the reforms, lingered and festered in some banks. These gave rise to crises that in 2008–09 eventually engulfed and threatened to bring down Nigeria's financial sector.

Governor Sanusi, in his speech of February 26, 2010, summarized it best. In his words, bank CEOs "set up Special Purpose Vehicles to lend money to themselves for stock price manipulation or the purchase of estates all over the world. One bank borrowed money and purchased private jets registered in the name of the CEO's son. In another bank, the management set up 100 fake companies for the purpose of perpetrating fraud. A lot of the capital supposedly raised by these so called mega banks was fake capital financed from depositors' funds. Thirty percent of the share capital of Intercontinental Bank was purchased with customer deposits. Afribank used depositors' funds to purchase 80 percent of its Initial Public Offering (IPO). It paid [25 naira] a share when the shares were trading at [11 naira] on the Nigerian Stock Exchange and these shares later collapsed to less than [3 naira]. The CEO of Oceanic Bank controlled over 35 percent of the bank through SPVs borrowing customer deposits."

The Nigerian financial system was thus in a delicate position when the global financial and economic crisis hit in 2008. Though it avoided the twin vulnerabilities of burgeoning private external debt and currency mismatches that were prevalent in many countries, it could not avoid the indirect effects of a sharp fall in the oil price and the flight to quality and safety that hit the stock market. The quality of banks' loan portfolios fell, and the stock-market bubble burst. Within a period of a few months in 2008, the price of Nigeria's main export, oil, fell from US\$146 a barrel to US\$40 a barrel. This impacted the second-tier and third-tier suppliers of goods and services in the sector and their ability to service their loans. In addition, the sharp decline in the Nigerian stock market by 68 percent from the February 2008 peak to December 2009 exposed the risky margin lending of many banks as their balance sheets were eroded. The lack of transparency in the disclosures of several other banks became clear as it emerged that a large proportion of the fastest-growing category of bank loans (finance, insurance, and general, accounting for 50 percent of lending) was really channeled into margin lending.

The Nigerian financial sector was in crisis, but the biggest source of its problems could be traced to five banks: Afribank, Finbank, Intercontinental Bank, Oceanic Bank, and Union Bank. Those five banks, accounting for about 40 percent of the country's bank credit, had 1.14 trillion naira (US\$7.6 billion) in bad loans, had very low cash reserves, and essentially depended on the CBN's discount window for continued support and operations.

Reforming the Banking Reforms

To clean up the mess in the banking sector, the CBN, led by Governor Sanusi, took quick and decisive action, injecting 400 billion naira (US\$2.6 billion) into the ailing banks. An additional 220 billion naira was injected into three more banks (Bank PHB, Spring Bank, and Wema Bank) as the crisis unfolded. The CEOs and management teams of the five most affected institutions were sacked, with prosecutions following. Recoveries were also made. The Economic and Financial Crimes Commission (EFCC) went after high-profile debtors as well as the creditors. EFCC claims to have recovered more than 46 billion naira in the exercise. Some of the bank executives (among them the CEO of Oceanic Bank, Cecilia Ibru) were made to forfeit assets (in her case up to 150 billion naira). The EFCC further secured a conviction against Ibru, and she served six months in jail. Other prosecutions are ongoing. A state-backed Asset Management Corporation was created to buy up bad loans.

The CBN introduced additional reforms, supposed to be rolled out over the decade. The four pillars of those reforms are as follows.

Enhancing the Quality of Banks This pillar consists of remedial programs focused on strengthening corporate governance, risk management, enforcement, data quality, and fighting financial crime. Quality enhancement will also include implementation of risk-based supervision, reforms to regulations and regulatory framework, enhanced provision for consumer protection, and internal transformation of the CBN.

Establishing Financial Stability This pillar focuses on strengthening the financial stability committee within the CBN and on developing hybrid monetary policy and macro-prudential rules. In this latter area, the rules focus on limiting capital market lending to a set proportion of a bank's balance sheet; prohibiting banks from using depositors' funds for proprietary trading, private equity, or venture capital investments; adjusting capital adequacy ratios depending on the perceived riskiness of the bank or financial institution; adjusting capital adequacy depending on the perceived point in the cycle; and establishing forward-looking capital requirements driven by stress tests conducted by the CBN.

Enabling Healthy Evolution of the Financial Sector This pillar focuses on reviewing the structure of the banking industry and that of credit bureaus and registrars, the cost structure of banks, and the role of the informal economy. The review of the industry's structure considers diversified mandates for banks that might involve international, national, regional, and monoline banks such as noninterest banking, with capital requirements varying with the range and the complexity of the mandate.

Ensuring That the Financial Sector Contributes to the Real Economy This pillar supports an advocacy role for the CBN in promoting a stronger linkage between the financial sector and the real economy, with the CBN supporting a strong role for the state in development finance, either by channeling resources through the banking sector or by directly supporting state sectoral institutions in such areas as agriculture, urban development, and housing.

Conclusion

The CBN's quick interventions in the banking sector, though fiscally costly, have led to stability, greater transparency, and the return of confidence to the sector, both nationally and internationally. The jury is still out on the long agenda of reforms designed to strengthen the sector and prepare it to be a major player in Nigeria's economy.

Some of the proposed reforms, such as the implementation of specialized banking—specifically, Islamic banking—are generating strong emotional reactions in Nigeria, where religion is susceptible to political manipulation, and thus must be handled carefully and in a more nuanced fashion. Hence the need to refer to non-interest forms of banking in the Nigerian context rather than the use of religious nomenclature. The CBN's supposed advocacy for a greater role for itself in the real sectors of the economy is also controversial. Though many support this, there are those who perceive the CBN as having stepped beyond advocacy into the role of a fiscal agent because of its ongoing direct and indirect support to various sectors, including agriculture and aviation. Despite the innovative structure of AMCON, with liabilities largely underwritten by the CBN, Banks, and the sale of distressed assets, there is some nervousness about the burgeoning size of it's balance sheet of problem assets and its potential impact on those who have to underwrite its operations. Ultimately, AMCON's liabilities are also contingent liabilities on the government's books but so far the judgment is that its operations are sound. In the end, the success of the reforms will be judged on persistence and consistency in implementation, with a focus on the changes that are needed to keep the financial sector open, transparent, and a sound pillar of the Nigerian economy.

5   Fighting Corruption

By the time we began the economic reform program, Nigeria had become virtually synonymous with the word "corruption." Unless we found a way to confront corruption and enhance transparency in our economic and social life in a consistent manner, we would not be able to convince Nigerians or the world that we were serious about reform. We had to move quickly, and we had to move far beyond generalities and platitudes. We needed to understand the corrosive nature of the corrupt acts being perpetrated, pinpoint which ones had the biggest impacts on the public finances or on institutions in the country, and then devise specific measures to fight these practices. We also needed clear metrics so we could see where we were having an effect and share that information with the public. The four stories that follow may help the reader to understand the nature of corruption in Nigeria and how it had struck at the very heart of the country, undermining prospects for development.

Corruption on a Grand Scale: Theft of Public Assets by High Public Officials

On September 15, 2005, Diepreye Alamieyeseigha, governor of the Nigerian state of Bayelsa, was arrested at London's Heathrow Airport and interrogated on allegations of money laundering by officers of the London Metropolitan Police's Specialist and Economic Crime Unit. From the airport he was taken to his home in the Paddington area of London. A search of the home resulted in the discovery of the equivalent of £920,000. On September 28, 2005, he was arraigned on three counts of money laundering. In addition to the monies discovered in his house, charges were brought against him for £420,000 found in his account and for illegally transferring another £475,000 to another account. In all, he was charged with laundering more than £1.8 million. The governor asserted his innocence. He was granted bail, pending trial. He then jumped bail and escaped from the UK disguised as a woman. He fled to Nigeria, where the constitution grants governors, presidents, and vice presidents immunity from prosecution while in office.

Nigeria's Economic and Financial Crimes Commission, under the leadership of Nuhu Ribadu (a star member of the Economic Team), had been investigating Alamieyeseigha for three years. Unable to prosecute him in Nigeria, the EFCC had collaborated with the Metropolitan Police to have him arrested and prosecuted in the UK, where he had exported some of the proceeds of the alleged money laundering. Though he could not be prosecuted in Nigeria, he could certainly be impeached. On November 24, 2005, about six weeks after his arrest, thousands of citizens of Bayelsa State staged a peaceful protest demanding his resignation or impeachment. The protest mirrored the mood of many Nigerians at the time—a mood nicely captured in a cartoon by Tayo Fatunla.

On December 12, 2005, nearly two months after his arrest, Governor Alamieyeseigha was impeached by his state's assembly. After losing his post and his immunity, he was arrested by the EFCC and the Nigerian police and successfully prosecuted for money laundering. He spent a brief time in jail. His was one of the first such high-level prosecutions by the EFCC, and it was an important signal that there could be no more impunity.

Governor Alamieyeseigha's money laundering was by no means an isolated case. Earlier in 2005, another governor had been arrested in London on similar charges and had managed to escape to Nigeria, also jumping bail. Indeed, the EFCC later reported that it was investigating 28 of Nigeria's 36 governors at the time on charges of corruption, theft of public funds, abuse of office, and money laundering. When out of office, five of these governors were arrested and charged by the EFCC. On the international level, collaboration between foreign authorities has resulted in cases still being pursued in London and in other jurisdictions. In at least one instance, associates of a former governor (James Ibori of Delta State) have been convicted in the UK. Ibori himself pleaded guilty in London to fraud and money laundering charges.

The significance of corruption charges against the governors was immense for Nigerian society, and huge for its ramifications for Nigeria's public finances. The Nigerian constitution requires that all

A cartoon, by Tayo Fatunla, depicting Governor Diepreye Alamieyeseigha and some Nigerian citizens.

revenues accruing to the Nigerian Federation be divided monthly in a predetermined formula between the Federal Government and other levels of government (the 36 state governments, and the Federal Capital Territory of Abuja, and 774 local governments). This ensures an almost 50–50 split of the revenues between the Federal Government and the subnational authorities. Thus, when Nigeria earned about US$25 billion from oil in 2004, half of that went to the state and local governments; when the amount jumped to US$45 billion the next year because of high oil prices, the subnational levels of government almost doubled their revenues. The governors of the states have almost complete autonomy in the constitution as to how to manage and use these resources. The states and the local governments are mandated to provide certain basic services: education, health, waste management, water, rural and state roads, and other state and municipal services. While I was in government (2003–2006), and earlier, Nigerians in most states had witnessed little improvement in service delivery from their state governments, and many services had in fact deteriorated. The people needed their money to be spent well on delivery of basic services. Diversion of state money was surely not the way to ensure this.

Corruption from the Top: Theft of Public Assets by a Former Dictator

Most accounts of corruption in Nigeria pale in comparison with the brazen corruption of General Sani Abacha, Nigeria's military ruler from 1993 to 1998. This story illustrates on a grander scale how corruption can undermine growth and poverty reduction in a nation's economy. In August 2004, authorities in Switzerland accepted the argument of Nigeria's lawyers that an Abacha-run criminal organization existed whose purpose was to engage in the looting and laundering of Nigerian public funds. After a hard-fought five-year battle to prove the criminal origin of monies corruptly acquired by the Abacha criminal organization, the Swiss government agreed to repatriate about US$505 million of frozen Abacha funds back to Nigeria in 2005 and 2006.[1] In the five years of Abacha's rule, an estimated US$3 billion to US$5 billion of Nigeria's public assets were looted and sent abroad by Abacha, his family, and their associates. These sums amounted to a substantial part of Nigeria's public assets—2.6 to 4.3 percent of the 2006 gross domestic product, and 20.6 to 34.4 percent of the 2006 federal budget. At the upper end of the range, the amount stolen is larger than the 2006 education and health federal budgets combined. According to cost estimates provided by the World Bank, that amount of money could provide anti-retroviral therapy for 2 million to 3 million people infected with HIV/AIDS over a ten-year period, or 200 million insecticide-treated bed nets.

Of the amount stolen, more than US$2.2 billion was carted away from the Central Bank of Nigeria in truckloads of cash in the form of foreign currency and travelers checks. Most of this money was laundered abroad through a complex network of companies, banks, and shell concerns before finding its way into foreign bank accounts operated by the Abacha family and their cronies. At the peak of these activities, more than 70 companies, and more than 32 banks—including some of the world's best-known banks—had money laundered through them. Figure A5.1 illustrates the complex schemes by which some of the Abacha money was laundered abroad with payments made from the Central Bank of Nigeria.

Another classic method of corruption practiced by the Abacha criminal organization involved contract inflation. One particularly odious case involved a Nigerian Family Support Program contract for Pasteur Mérieux vaccines—a program that was designed to benefit poor families, especially poor women and children. The US$111 million contract was awarded to Morgan Procurement Ltd., a company belonging to the Abacha family. The true value of the vaccines was US$22.5 million. Essentially, US$88.5 million was skimmed off as profit for the family and transferred to their various accounts. This subversion of the country's vaccines procurement introduced corruption into a crucial health program. It became virtually systemic and greatly undermined the country's immunization and vaccination program, which in turn harmed Nigerian children.

Corruption from Within: Corruption by Foreign Companies and Their Domestic Partners in Crime

Foreign companies have been involved in some of the worst cases of corruption in developing countries. Nigeria is replete with accounts of such corrupt and corrupting behavior by foreign companies. The recent admission by the global engineering giant Siemens of corrupt payments in Nigeria and elsewhere illustrates just how difficult and how pervasive this problem is. Siemens, to its credit, admitted paying 10 million euros to Nigerian government officials between 2001 and 2004 to facilitate contract awards. The company has cooperated in providing information when asked, and has revamped its approach to doing business in Nigeria and its corporate culture.[2]

This third story of corruption by a foreign company in Nigeria has been well documented in the *Financial Times* and in other international newspapers.[3] It involves a lucrative oil and gas project. Sometime in 1994, the TSKJ consortium (comprising France's Technip, Italy's Snamprogetti, the Halliburton subsidiary Kellogg Brown & Root, and Japan's JGC) made a bid to provide services to a US$12 billion liquefied natural gas project in Nigeria partly owned by the Nigerian government and the Royal Dutch Shell group. This initial bid was not accepted. Subsequently, the TSKJ group obtained the services of Tristar Investments, a separate company, which was to provide "consultancy" services to enable the company to win the contract in the LNG project. In December of 1995, TSKJ was awarded a US$2 billion contract for the Nigerian LNG project. Years later, evidence was produced that the TSKJ group had internally discussed making payments of about US$180 million to various foreign accounts of Nigerian officials to help TSKJ obtain its lucrative contract. Nigerians collectively pay the price of such bribery through inflated contracts and undermining of the country's institutions.

Corruption from the Bottom: Private Intimidation

This fourth story is a bit different from the others, but no less worrying because of its insidious impact on Nigeria's society and basic institutions. It is the tale of Rose, a 21-year-old university student who was the first child in her family to leave her rural village and receive a university education. She could not afford to purchase the class notes that her lecturer sold to students. The lecturer, who used the monies obtained by selling the notes to supplement his income, noticed that Rose was not purchasing the notes and penalized her with low grades. When she explained that she could not pay for the notes in cash, she was invited to pay by rendering other services. She refused and got a failing grade. She became terribly demoralized. She felt alone and isolated and eventually withdrew from the university, thus putting an end to her higher education and the dreams of her family and her village, who had seen in her education a path to escape poverty.

When I followed up on this story, I found that it was by no means an isolated case. Young Nigerians and their relatives told me many similar stories. A systemic rot has befallen Nigeria's once-solid system of public tertiary education. Similar tales abound of public health workers asking for under-the-table payments for services and diverting hospital supplies, drugs, and equipment to their private clinics. Nigeria is bedeviled by very poor provision of public services in education and health, largely because of corruption and undermining of institutions by a small percentage of the population.

How Did We Fight Back?

It was clear to the Economic Team working on the reforms that fighting corruption successfully would require four crucial and inseparable ingredients. The first was political will and commitment from the very top. The second was specificity in terms of identifying the most damaging forms of corruption and focusing on those. The third was developing measurable indicators of success or other means of demonstrating success. We strongly believed that the more the Nigerian public could see a serious, successful fight against corruption, the more they would own this fight and demand that it continue. Finally, we needed the ability to withstand personal intimidation or threats, and to forge on with the fight.

Maintaining Political Will
President Obasanjo demonstrated in his first administration and at the beginning of the reform program that he understood that fighting corruption was central to the economic well-being and development of the country. He created two institutions that would take the lead in investigating corrupt practices and bringing perpetrators to justice: the Independent Corrupt Practices and Other Offenses Commission (ICPC) in his first term, and the Economic and Financial Crimes Commission in his second term. The president understood that he would not be able to realize one of the main objectives of his administration—obtaining debt relief—unless Nigerian authorities were seen to be serious about fighting corruption. No creditors would want to forgive or cancel any debts if they believed that the proceeds of cancellation would end up in corrupt hands. For much of the duration of the reform program, the president gave his backing; his support wavered as new presidential

elections approached and politicians gained more influence over the president.

Focusing Efforts, Devising Indicators of Success, and Enhancing Transparency

The Economic Team concluded that the most damaging form of corruption for the economy was theft of public assets, either through outright diversion of public revenues into private hands at the local, state, and federal levels or through inflated contracts. If we could devise means to block this theft, it would have a strong effect on other sources and types of corruption.

To bring greater transparency to our public finances, I published the revenues accruing to each level of government monthly in national newspapers. This was an instant success because people could see just how much their local government chairman or their state governor received in transfers that month. They began to ask why teachers were not being paid in schools, why there was no chalk in the classrooms, why potholes were not repaired, and why rubbish wasn't removed. The publication of revenues put information in the hands of citizens and put the government officials—particularly the governors—on the defensive.

To make government finances even more transparent and entrench better management of public resources, we developed a Fiscal Responsibility Law, which required the Federal Government and the states to develop, pass, and publish annually their budgets, with full justification of development expenditures, and with an annual review of the performance of these budgets. The law also introduced restrictions on state borrowing and implemented an oil-price-based fiscal rule that de-linked the budget from the oil price and allowed the government to save in times of high oil prices. It could then use these savings to buttress revenues in times of low oil prices. Much of the legislation was later watered down by the states, using arguments about the law's constitutionality to evade some of its strictures.

Another colleague on the team, Oby Ezekwesili, mapped out a methodology for reviewing government contracts and assessing their unit costs against a database compiled from information on the Internet. This analysis showed that the unit cost of Nigerian contracts was sometimes four times that of contracts in neighboring Ghana. This type of analysis, accompanied by requirements for local and international competitive bidding of contracts, became popularly known as the "due process" methodology. Over two and a half years, the approach saved Nigeria an estimated US$1.5 billion by reining in inflated contracts that would have depleted public resources. In time, a "due process" office was created that then became the Bureau for Public Procurement, and legislation was passed to institutionalize the approach.

The Economic Team also began to take a concerted look at corruption in the oil and gas sector, where corruption was deeply entrenched, as most Nigerians believed and the TSKJ story corroborated. Oby Eze-kwesili and Bright Okogu enrolled Nigeria in the Extractive Industries Transparency Initiative, an international initiative designed to bring greater transparency to the extractive sector. (See box 5.1.)

Box 5.1
Monitoring Resource Riches: The Extractive Industries Transparency Initiative

The Extractive Industries Transparency Initiative (EITI) is a voluntary global initiative consisting of a set of standards to promote revenue transparency and accountability in resource-rich countries. The standards require companies to publish what they pay and governments to disclose revenues from oil, gas, and mining. The EITI Board and the international secretariat are responsible for maintaining the global standards, while participating countries are responsible for implementation. EITI was launched in 2002 at the Johannesburg World Summit for Sustainable Development by Tony Blair, then Prime Minister of the UK. As of May 2009, EITI has been implemented in about 30 resource-rich countries around the world.

In 2003, Nigeria became one of the first countries to adopt the EITI. Together with Azerbaijan and Ghana, it has piloted the EITI approach. The Nigeria Extractive Industries Transparency Initiative (NEITI) bill was approved in May 2007. NEITI functions through the National Stakeholders Working Group, which has representatives from the government, civil society, private-sector companies, and extractive industry experts. One of NEITI's main activities was the financial, physical, and process audit of the domestic petroleum sector from 1999 to 2004. The audit results identified some of the shortcomings in the sector, and the results were widely disseminated to all stakeholders:

• The physical audit pointed to the loss of crude oil between the oil wellhead and the export metering terminals. The poor metering infrastructure also prevented accurate collection of data on output volumes.
• The process audit revealed deficiencies in management, leading to a capacity utilization of only 47 percent in the refineries, for example.

Source: Okonjo-Iweala and Osafo-Kwaako 2007.

Under the Extractive Industries Transparency Initiative, companies in the extractive sector must publish what they pay governments in taxes, royalties, and other fees, and governments must publish what they receive, so the two can be compared. Nigeria's EITI effort went far beyond that. The Nigeria EITI (NEITI) included process, financial, and physical audits of the oil sector's upstream and downstream activities in what became known as EITI++. The audits revealed discrepancies in reported physical quantities and financial accounts, and led the government to investigate the sources of these discrepancies more deeply.

The efforts to increase transparency and improve economic and financial approaches were complemented by improvements to investigative and punitive measures through the work of the Economic and Financial Crimes Commission (EFCC). For too long, corrupt officials and their associates had acted with impunity in their corrupt dealings; for any fight to be successful, impunity had to be reined in. The Independent Corrupt Practices Commission (ICPC), also set up by President Obasanjo in his first term, played an active role. The EFCC, under Nuhu Ribadu, was courageous and totally committed to tracking down corrupt officials. It initiated investigations of 28 governors and other associates. Once the governors left office, five were successfully arraigned before the courts on July 16, 2007, and two were tried and convicted. For the first time in Nigeria's history, the highest law officer of the land, the Inspector General of Police, was investigated for corruption, tried, convicted, and sentenced to six months in prison. Several ministers, judges, and civil servants were dismissed or suspended, and the president of the senate resigned, all as a result of various corruption scandals and investigations pushed by the EFCC and the ICPC.

The EFCC also set out to hunt down and punish the perpetrators of another pernicious form of corruption: the Internet scam known as "419," after section 419 of Nigeria's penal code. This scam, said to have originated in Nigeria and now copied in other countries, involves an e-mail message purporting that the sender is willing to share a business deal worth lots of money with the recipient provided the recipient sends the scammer money or a bank account number up front. Many people in developed countries and in emerging market countries have fallen victim to this scam, and it had badly tainted Nigeria's reputation abroad. The EFCC arrested and prosecuted several 419 kingpins. They were tried and jailed. Between 2003 and 2007, under the leadership of

Nuhu Ribadu, the EFCC obtained 270 convictions and recovered billions of naira.

Internationally, we deployed yet another corruption-fighting approach to complement the EFCC's domestic work. Nigeria cooperated with Switzerland, the UK, and other countries in an international effort to recover its public assets stolen and stashed abroad. President Obasanjo led this effort, working with General Aliyu Gusau, with Peter Gana, and with colleagues from a special police panel that was investigating assets looted under the Abacha regime. A committed Swiss law firm, Monfrini and Associates, worked with the relevant Swiss authorities.

Essentially, we recognized that there are two sides to the equation of theft and export of stolen public monies. There is the "sending country" from which the assets are stolen, but there is also the "receiving country," where various banks, shell companies, accountants, lawyers, and others who assist in laundering and sequestering money are located. The idea was that if we could get the countries whose financial institutions were harboring this money to cooperate and facilitate the return of the monies, this would demonstrate to those sending stolen assets abroad that there was no place to hide and would serve as a powerful complementary deterrent to public corruption and theft. The approach yielded some dividends.

From 2004 to 2006, I participated in the recovery of US$505 million of Abacha-looted funds. After a complicated legal battle, the Swiss federal government did the right thing and agreed to return the funds. They demanded and we accepted that we indicate how the returned monies would be spent. This was not without controversy among the Nigerian public, given that the money was Nigeria's. The Swiss authorities also requested that we work with the World Bank and with representatives of Nigerian and Swiss civil society to track expenditures and report on their use. With the assent of President Obasanjo, we indicated to the Swiss that returned Abacha monies would be used for incremental funding of activities related to achieving the Millennium Development Goals.

With the Swiss federal government indicating that the money could be returned sometime in 2004, I mapped out a plan for integrating the funds within the 2004 budget process. I flew to Switzerland on two occasions to discuss how these funds would be used to finance MDG-related activities in health, education, and rural infrastructure programs. Repatriation of the funds did not occur in 2004 as promised, so we had to float domestic bonds to cover the gap created in the budget. These were subsequently repaid when the funds were repatriated in 2005–06. The World Bank, working with non-governmental organizations and in the context of its regular Public Expenditure Review of December 2006, undertook a review of these expenditures, which focused on the financing of basic services such as rural electrification, water, and roads. (See table A5.1.) The review found that the funds had generally been directed to increased budget spending on the MDGs in the areas promised, although there were concerns related to tracking the quality and quantity of spending.

Later on, after I left Nigeria in 2006 to go as a fellow to the Brookings Institution in Washington—at the request of Paul Wolfowitz, then president of the World Bank, and later with the encouragement of Robert Zoellick, his successor as World Bank president—I worked to bring about the creation of the Stolen Asset Recovery (StAR) initiative, a joint endeavor of the World Bank and the United Nations Office on Drugs and Crime (UNODC) to help developing countries recover their plundered assets.

Withstanding Threats and Attacks

The bid to increase the transparency of government revenues and expenditures, to improve public procurement, and to intensify the scrutiny of major sectors of the economy, including oil and gas, together with the implementation of punitive measures on corruption, earned the reform team powerful enemies among the political elite. There were direct threats to various team members, including me. There were orchestrated attacks and smear campaigns in the media, and there was a fierce effort to undermine the reforms and the reformers. One area in which the anti-corruption fight could not make headway was the reform of the Nigerian Customs Service, widely regarded by many as an agency in need of clean-up, modernization, and reform. My attempts to reform it were undermined by the Custom Service's elite beneficiaries, who conducted a media campaign suggesting that foreigners were about to be brought in to take over and re-colonize the Customs Service. (See chapter 4.)

To quote my colleague Nuhu Ribadu, "When you fight corruption, corruption fights back." Corruption did fight back, and continues to do so long after we left office. But this did not deter the resolve of those of us working to reform the economy.

Measuring Results

How did we measure success? Right from the start, we were conscious of the need for metrics to capture progress and the effects of fighting corruption. We looked at both external and internal indicators of success. The first was Nigeria's position on the Transparency International Corruption Perceptions Index, an international benchmark measuring the perceived level and types of corruption in more than 150 countries.[4] When we started, in 2003, Nigeria was second to last after Bangladesh on the index. The objective was to move Nigeria up two to three notches within two years. By 2005, Nigeria, admittedly still in the wrong neighborhood, was nevertheless sixth from the bottom.

The second indicator was data from the Worldwide Governance Indicators published by the World Bank Institute (the Kaufman/Kraay index).[5] The KK 2005 survey data indicated a reduction in the perception of corruption by Nigerian firms in obtaining trade permits, paying taxes, in procurement, in the judiciary, in the leakage of public funds, and in money laundering, as shown in figure A5.2.

Third, on the financial side, progress was measured in terms of the monies saved by the Due Process Office from public contracts (US$1.5 billion over two years), and the US$500 million repatriated from Switzerland. In addition, the Economic and Financial Crimes Commission recovered several billion naira domestically. The EFCC's convictions were an important measure of success, especially for the Nigerian public. The continued popularity and demand for monthly publication in the newspapers of government revenues for all tiers of government signified public support for the efforts.

Conclusion

The integration of the anti-corruption fight into the center of Nigeria's economic reform program was unprecedented, as were the measurable results recorded by this fight. The effort was not without controversy, as some insisted that the EFCC's work, in particular, was politically motivated. There was, however, a consensus that courageous work had been done that had shifted the country's corruption landscape against the corrupt for the first time. This had a big effect on the average Nigerian, paving the way for greater intolerance of the corruption that had been undermining the country's development.

6   Obtaining Debt Relief

Debt relief was central to Nigeria's reform effort. Not only did it give the country breathing room to pursue other reforms; it also put it on a more sustainable footing for the future. The results were far better than anyone might have expected: a 60 percent write-off on Nigeria's official government (Paris Club) debt. What were the ingredients in this remarkable success, and how can the lessons be applied to other countries or similar campaigns? This chapter traces the background, issues, and elements that led to this success, including the roles played by various parties, among them representatives of civil society.

Nigeria approached its quest for relief strategically, flexibly, and pragmatically, using a combination of tested and new instruments. At the core of its strategy was its ability to craft a homegrown reform program and to deliver measurable successes on it, thus engendering credibility and trust with its partners and creditors. This was accompanied by effective technical and political footwork.

Debt relief for Nigeria can be seen as one of the most striking and sustained achievements of a remarkable three-year reform effort that turned the Nigerian economy around. For me, it was the culmination of three years of extremely hard work that was technically, intellectually, and emotionally testing—but also exhilarating. Shortly after I was sworn in as Nigeria's Minister of Finance, on July 17, 2003, I received a letter from President Olusegun Obasanjo stipulating that one of the items I had to deliver during my tenure was Paris Club debt relief for Nigeria. The president had made obtaining Paris Club debt relief both a personal and a national priority, and his instructions placed me squarely at the center of this daunting challenge. The president had campaigned for such debt relief in his first term (1999–2003) without success. He was therefore more determined to do whatever was needed to get rid of the debt in his second term. I was to be his instrument to achieve this. I knew that delivering would require drawing on many resources, including the hard work of the excellent Economic Team that President Obasanjo had assembled and that I led.

About two years later, on June 29, 2005, Nigeria and the Paris Club reached an historic agreement on the write-off of some US$18 billion in debt. The agreement was implemented from October 2005 to March 2006. Table A6.1 sets out the milestones in the colorful Nigerian debt saga, beginning in 1964 with the country's first external loan and ending in 2007 with the signing into law of Nigeria's Fiscal Responsibility Law.

Setting the Scene for Debt Relief

From 1964, when it took its first loan from the Paris Club of creditor countries,[1] to 1970, Nigeria borrowed moderately, despite the fact that it experienced a devastating civil war from 1967 to 1970. In 1970, at the end of the war, Nigeria's external debt was less than US$1 billion.

The situation changed dramatically during the oil boom of 1971–1981. Despite the high oil revenues, Nigeria's leaders borrowed unsustainably to finance postwar reconstruction and other state projects and infrastructure, perhaps convinced of the country's strong creditworthiness by those hawking loans. By 1985, Nigeria had accumulated an external debt of US$19 billion. A great deal of this money was from export credit agencies of Paris Club members and commercial banks for projects ranging from road construction to the development of manufacturing and agriculture, as well as the building of health clinics and water projects.

Unfortunately, many of these projects were either not implemented at all (the money disappeared completely) or were poorly implemented with very poor results, leading to a situation of high external indebtedness with less than commensurate results.[2] For example, the Arochukwu-Ohafia water project in Abia State, for which £12,360,000 was borrowed from a British creditor, was never implemented, and the loan could not be accounted for. In another instance, the Ihiala carpet manufacturing project in Anambra State took a loan of £10 million (€13.1 million), but the project was never delivered by the contracting companies. Instead, the companies were alleged to have participated in diversion of the loans into the private accounts of senior government officials, and some of them were later indicted. The Nigerian people were left to repay loans for projects that had never been built or that never delivered.

Given the prevailing high interest rates of the 1980s, debt service climbed to US$4 billion per year—the equivalent of 33 percent of exports of goods and services as of 1985. (The recommended international norm was 25 percent.) This by itself should not have been a serious problem; a conservative estimate of Nigeria's oil wealth at the time was US$75 billion, as against its external debt of US$19 billion. But because the economy had been badly mismanaged during the oil boom years, it became hostage to oil, with the agricultural sector completely devastated.[3] With the country growing at a low rate of 1 percent per year and oil accounting for the lion's share of government revenues, Nigeria entered an era when it was unable to service its loans as oil prices crashed. To ease the situation, the country sought rescheduling of its obligations, and four successive Paris Club reschedulings took place (in 1986, 1989, 1991, and 2000). However, relief was only temporary, and arrears began to mount, including interest and penalties on interest. During discussions that preceded the 1989 and 1991 rescheduling, Nigeria sought substantive relief based on new Paris Club initiatives, such as the 1994 Naples terms, designed to provide low-income qualifying countries with up to two-thirds flow or stock relief. However, this was denied. This refusal by creditor governments was in contrast to the agreement reached with the London Club of commercial creditors to consolidate and treat private debt arrears and obligations under the Brady Plan in 1991.[4]

By the mid 1990s, under the Sani Abacha regime, relationships with the Paris Club hit a low point and Nigeria suspended its repayments of interest and principle on Paris Club debt. In 1998, a transition military regime came into power, and an attempt was made to revive relations with the Paris Club by making a goodwill payment of US$1.5 billion. However, it was only in 1999, under the democratically elected regime of President Obasanjo, that the debt issue once more took center stage as the president campaigned for debt relief. By December 31, 2004, when external debts were being reconciled for the negotiations, Nigeria's external debt stood at US$35.994 billion, of which 86 percent, or US$30.9 billion, was owed to the Paris Club. Figure A6.1 shows Paris Club debt outstanding by creditor category before debt relief. Figure A6.2 displays the debt stock by creditor.

Total debt service stood at approximately US$3 billion a year, of which about US$2.3 billion was owed to the Paris Club, with the balance of US$0.7 billion owed to other multilateral and commercial creditors. In reality, however, only US$1 billion in Paris Club debt service was being implemented under a tacit agreement with the Club. Had Nigeria undertaken the full Paris Club annual debt service, it would have left the Federal Government with little or no budget for capital expenditures, so some accommodation was reached with the Club in 2000 on a temporary basis.

Payment arrears continued to mount. It was imperative that a fundamental and sustainable solution be found to the debt problem. To do this, we had to craft a strategy that would deliver on the Paris Club's fundamental criteria for debt relief while mobilizing essential constituencies and individuals in Paris Club creditor countries to support Nigeria's cause.

Let me now turn to the subject of the fundamental criteria.

Navigating Paris Club Debt Relief: Fundamental Elements

To be considered for Paris Club debt relief, Nigeria had to meet some fundamental criteria of the Club, most of which it was not well positioned to meet in 2003. At the time, the country was experiencing considerable macroeconomic instability and weak growth in the run-up to 2003, as evidenced in the economic indicators presented in table A6.2.

Paris Club debt relief of the sort Nigeria desired—that is, involving a substantial debt write-off—would require attaining a number of difficult and mutual preconditions:

• implementation of economic reforms under a formal program approved by the International Monetary Fund (IMF)

• eligibility of the country for borrowing from the "soft loan" or concessional arm of the World Bank reserved for the poorest countries—that is, IDA-only borrowing status (IDA standing for International Development Association)[5]

• regularization of debt service or establishment of a good debt-service record

• meeting the threshold of the IMF–World Bank Debt Sustainability Analysis (DSA), which would indicate that the country's debt was not sustainable in the long term and could ultimately severely undermine growth.

For each of these criteria, Nigeria faced a challenge for different reasons. Each of the challenges had to be met with a solution.

Implementation of an Economic Reform Program Approved by the IMF

The implementation of a formal economic reform program approved by the IMF was a major hurdle. From the mid 1980s to the early 1990s, Nigerians had developed strong negative feelings about adjustment programs led by the IMF and the World Bank, and had indicated, in what was tantamount to an informal national referendum, that they wanted no truck with IMF programs. Even if a program were to exist, Nigerians did not want to draw on IMF resources.

How, then, could the president or the new Economic Team convince Nigerians to accept a formal IMF economic reform program? We decided that we could not, especially because there was already a suspicion that people like me who came from these institutions would try to force the country into such a program.

Instead, the new Economic Team came up with another approach: the idea of crafting a homegrown economic reform program by Nigerians, for Nigerians. It would be at least as strong as a program the IMF would have put in place. Having implemented it, Nigeria would invite the IMF to monitor its progress in the hope and expectation that such an approach would be acceptable to the Paris Club. Thus, the Economic Team developed the National Economic Empowerment and Development Program (NEEDS), which sought to tackle a number of economic problems simultaneously. It would stabilize the macroeconomy, fight corruption, bring transparency to government business, strengthen fiscal policy, improve the management of the budget, privatize inefficient state assets, liberalize certain essential sectors, and implement public service reform and financial-sector restructuring. (See chapters 1–4.) The program was comprehensive and touched on all the major areas in which Nigeria had serious economic problems. The program was result-oriented and featured a matrix that set targets and results, including responsibilities and accountabilities for such results.

For the first time, we had a reform program that was owned and crafted by Nigerians for themselves. The IMF was formally invited to monitor its implementation, and it accepted. This was uncharted territory for the IMF, but there was no good reason why it should not accept to work with a country that was determined to do the right thing. The IMF and World Bank teams responsible for Nigeria at the time were smart, confident, good listeners, and excellent partners, and they recommended to their management that they form a partnership with us in the way requested.[6]

Menachem Katz, the IMF's mission leader for Nigeria, was instrumental in persuading senior managers at the IMF, such as Anne Krueger, the first deputy managing director, to support Nigeria's proposed new approach to working with the IMF. We were extremely lucky that they were willing to listen and support us, as the Bretton Woods institutions, especially the IMF, did not always have the reputation of "thinking outside the box." Anne Krueger at the IMF, Jim Wolfensohn, president of the World Bank, and several managers and staff below them became staunch supporters. Chief among them was Hafez Ghanem, the World Bank country director based in Nigeria. Despite the opposition of vested interests, Nigerians generally accepted the reform program, and we successfully implemented it for more than 15 months, stabilizing the macroeconomy, growing the non-oil sector, and increasing reserves (as shown in table A6.3) before approaching the Group of Eight and the Paris Club to request consideration for debt relief.

Ultimately, the Paris Club insisted that this approach was too informal and could set "dangerous" precedents for other countries wishing to negotiate with it in the future. It insisted that some way be found to capture Nigeria's program under a more formal IMF instrument. By sheer coincidence, at the fall and spring meetings of the IMF and the World Bank in 2004 and 2005, discussions centered on creating a new IMF instrument for countries that wanted IMF oversight of their programs but did not need access to IMF resources. Nigeria's situation fit this bill exactly. We lobbied IMF senior management, developing country finance ministers of the Group of Twenty-Four,[7] and developed country treasuries to support the creation of the new instrument—with Nigeria the first country to test it. I recall asking Francisco Gil-Diaz, Mexico's finance minister, to help me persuade G24 ministers, especially those from Latin America, to support Nigeria's quest to pilot test the new instrument. He was very successful in doing that.

When created, the instrument was called the Policy Support Instrument (PSI). Nigeria was the first country whose homegrown program was encapsulated in a PSI and taken to the IMF Board. The board approved the program in September 2005, thus paving the way for final Paris Club negotiations and implementation of the debt-relief agreements.

Eligibility for IDA-Only Status at the World Bank

At the January 2004 World Economic Forum in Davos, Switzerland, Nancy Birdsall—president of a Washington-based think tank, the

Center for Global Development (CGD), and a former colleague of mine at the World Bank—asked me why Nigeria was not eligible for the Heavily Indebted Poor Countries (HIPC) initiative.[8] Why wasn't Nigeria classified as a country eligible to borrow only from the soft loan arm of the Bank (the International Development Association), she wondered, given that it had all the income characteristics and human-development indicators of IDA-only countries? Nigeria was classified by the World Bank as being eligible to borrow both from the IDA and from the regular window of the Bank, the International Bank for Reconstruction and Development (IBRD), meaning that it was considered more creditworthy than IDA-only countries. This automatically made it difficult, if not impossible, for the Paris Club to consider Nigeria for any substantial debt relief that initiatives, such as the Naples terms, accorded highly indebted low-income countries. Yet for 12 years the World Bank had not allowed Nigeria access to any IBRD lending. So a contradictory situation emerged: Nigeria, because of its access to oil revenues, was classified as entitled to access to non-concessional IBRD borrowing in theory; yet in practice, because of its actual low creditworthiness, Nigeria had been restricted from any IBRD borrowing for more than a decade. Nancy and I discussed the unfairness of this situation and the unfairness of the result: the lack of a level playing field for Nigeria and other countries.

The Center for Global Development prepared a policy paper on the issue, which was disseminated to the World Bank and to other audiences likely to have some influence on the Paris Club process. At the same time, I formally approached the World Bank to correct this anomaly and make Nigeria IDA-only. The World Bank's president, Jim Wolfensohn, and its managing director, Shengman Zhang, were sympathetic, but we had to overcome the objections of those in the Bank's finance complex who felt that Nigeria was undeserving—and who, in any event, thought Nigeria might request a large slice of IDA funds if made IDA-only. In their thinking, this would undercut the access of other smaller countries to IDA.

I needed to offer assurances—and credible ones. I promised that if made IDA-only, Nigeria would not request access to a larger share of IDA resources than what was already programmed. We were interested in this only for the purposes of meeting the Paris Club's requirement of IDA-only status for Naples terms or other deep-discount debt-relief arrangements. With the strong support of the Bank's country director for Nigeria, Hafez Ghanem, and his team, a case was made and approved within the Bank for IDA-only status for Nigeria based on tangible results in important areas: improved economic performance, a strong fight against corruption, and poor social indicators.

Regularizing Debt Service

In the mid 1980s, Nigeria's ability to service its Paris Club debt began to deteriorate. By 1985, when the debt-service payment due had grown to US$4 billion, Nigeria was able to pay only US$1.5 billion. The four Paris Club reschedulings that followed did not solve the problem, as the country quickly fell behind again in the context of the low commodity price of its main export—oil—and its need for basic expenditures during this period. Nigeria did faithfully service its remaining London Club debt, as well as its multilateral obligations, given the good treatment it had received at the hands of London Club creditors and the seniority of multilateral debt service. Yet all the while, arrears, penalties, and interest accrued on its Paris Club debt service, giving Nigeria a poor track record with the Club. Compounding this was the lack of a real dialogue between the parties in the 1990s.

Starting in 2000, when I was first invited by President Obasanjo to help sort out Nigeria's tangled debt situation, regular dialogue was restored. The creation of the Debt Management Office and the cleaning up of debt data provided a basis for the restarting of the dialogue. The Paris Club reschedulings of 1989, 1991, and 2000 had lengthened Nigeria's repayment period and lowered the debt-service amount from the 1985 level.

Yet paying the lower amount (about US$2.3 billion) was still a problem. The service of Paris Club debt fell mainly on Nigeria's Federal Government budget, which was around $US9 billion in 2002. The full debt-service payment of US$2.3 billion for the Paris Club, plus another US$0.7 billion for the London Club and multilaterals (US$3 billion in all), would have amounted to about five times Nigeria's education budget and more than ten times its federal health budget. Politically, this was extremely difficult to defend; hence the need to negotiate for a realistic US$1 billion of annual debt service for the Paris Club. The trick was then to maintain this informal agreement to establish good faith and create a reasonable track record. With one breach (in 2002, an election year), Nigeria was able to keep to this informal, unwritten agreement, thereby restoring a level of regularization to its debt-service record. Thus Nigeria was gradually able to restore its credibility—a valuable asset when it came time to ask for further support. Nigeria increasingly became a country on whose word the outside world could rely.

Dealing with Debt Sustainability Analyses and Thresholds

A crucial part of the Paris Club process to decide whether to grant countries debt relief and to determine the measure of relief to be granted is based on IMF and World Bank analyses that establish whether a country's debt is sustainable. Debt Sustainability Analyses (DSAs) assess whether a country can comfortably service its Paris Club debt given its level and pattern of growth, its export levels and potential (which measures ability to earn foreign exchange), its revenue and expenditure levels, and projections into the future of all these factors. The two institutions establish certain debt ratios based on these DSAs, which serve as benchmarks against which a country's debt-sustainability situation can be measured and projected into the future. Examples are the ratio of debt to gross domestic product, the ratio of debt service to exports, and the ratio of debt service to revenues. Table A6.4 provides the indicative norms for these ratios. If a country falls within these norms, it can service its debts and the debt burden is deemed to be sustainable. If it doesn't, the degree of unsustainability is examined for decisions as to whether the country's debt should be rescheduled to give it breathing room until its finances are more robust and it can resume regular debt service, or whether a deeper type of debt relief or write-off should be considered.

Developing countries have protested that these ratios fail to take into account many factors that capture their actual situations. For example, most developing countries have domestic debt that must be serviced; the typical DSA does not take this into account, often making ratios look more optimistic than should be the case. On the basis of these criticisms, the World Bank and the IMF have attempted to refine their methodologies, and the DSA has improved, but issues still remain, as we argued in Nigeria's case.

Nigeria was seeking debt relief at the end of 2004, when the price of its main export commodity, oil, was increasing. Oil prices had risen from a per barrel average of US$28.9 in 2003 to US$37.8 in 2004, and had shot to US$53.4 in 2005. Many analysts projected continued increases in oil prices, and Paris Club members were in no mood to entertain debt relief for a so-called oil-rich country whose commodity price was robust. But what seemed to be forgotten was that oil prices had fallen as low as US$10 per barrel only a few years earlier. *The Economist* had famously predicted in its March 1999 issue that they were headed down to US$5 per barrel. Similar volatility occurred in 2008, with oil prices reaching US$146 a barrel by the middle of the year and falling below US$45 a barrel by the year's end.

Allowing for the unpredictable volatility of oil prices is important not only for reaching and sticking to a sustainable path for debt, but also for the equally important goal of having an economy less dependent on oil and capable of steady, fast growth. This would be in contrast to the ruinous ups and downs that have characterized many oil-exporting developing countries, including Nigeria.

Two implications mentioned in chapter 2 are worth restating. First, if oil prices are capable of large movements both up and down, it makes little sense to base either public spending plans or an assessment of creditworthiness on the prevailing oil price; it is far better to use some long-run average. Second, oil revenues differ from traditional tax revenues in that they involve depleting a national asset that cannot be replaced. Therefore, special care must be taken to ensure that oil revenues are spent wisely to build up durable long-run assets whose benefits can be shared with future generations. Using a conservative reference price for oil instead of its current price for government budgeting goes a long way toward dealing with its volatility and exhaustibility. It dampens volatility, which makes the economic environment more stable for non-oil-sector investments, enables a savings cushion to be built up during oil-price booms, and bolsters credibility by signaling that oil revenues are not going to be squandered—the latter being especially important for oil-exporting countries that have a bad history to overcome.

With the price of oil above US$50 per barrel in 2005, the standard DSA showed that Nigeria's debt could be sustainable on the basis of prevailing oil-price forecasts. But the standard analysis could not capture Nigeria's true situation, given the realities of volatility, depletion of a natural resource, and need for diversification of the economic base. We had to get those elements on the table. Just as the price of oil could keep rising, it could also fall dramatically. If the latter happened, Nigeria's situation could quickly become unsustainable. Any DSA for Nigeria would have to factor in a downside as well as an upside. In addition, Nigeria had a substantial domestic debt burden of about US$10 billion, with annual debt service at US$1.4 billion at the time. It also had contingent pension liabilities and other liabilities.

Most important, however, was the issue of how Nigeria could meet the development targets set by the international community as crucial for poverty reduction and improved human development—the Millennium Development Goals—while still sustainably servicing its Paris Club debt. Nigeria, like most other African countries, was off target for meeting the MDGs and would need substantial investments in education, health, and basic infrastructure (such as water, rural roads, and electricity) to make substantial progress toward meeting the goals by 2015.

The push by the international community to get developing countries to work toward meeting the MDGs, on the one hand, while insisting on debt service, on the other, seemed to me to be more and more contradictory and hypocritical. On a given day, we would meet with officials from the aid departments of our creditor countries of the Paris Club and they would speak about the need to invest effectively to meet the MDGs. Yet on the same day, officials from the treasuries of those countries would also demand that we meet the debt payments. It was clear that the two sides were not talking to each other; had they been talking, they would have realized that Nigeria would not be able to do both.

We decided that this crucial factor of investment for the MDGs had somehow to be factored into the thinking on the Debt Sustainability Analysis. This would indeed be revolutionary thinking by Paris Club standards. The very idea of a DSA with the MDGs factored in was scary to the treasuries of Nigeria's creditor countries. We were warned informally by the Paris Club Secretariat in Paris, who got wind of what we were contemplating, that Paris Club members would reject this approach because it could set a precedent for other countries.

We nevertheless proceeded and asked the World Bank to work with us to analyze what Nigeria's DSA would look like if investments needed for the MDGs were factored in. Our reasoning was simple. Nigeria received one of the lowest amounts of aid in the developing world: US$2 per capita per year, compared with US$28 per capita per year for sub-Saharan African countries. In actuality, with its annual debt service of US$1.7 billion, Nigeria was sending out more money to the developed world than it received: the net transfer per capita per year was US$11. If Nigeria was to make MDG investments while continuing with the high Paris Club debt service, financing would have to come from its own resources. Alternatively, Nigeria would have to borrow afresh to invest, which would not be a sustainable situation.

The IMF team worked informally with the World Bank team headed by Brian Pinto to weave the MDGs into the DSA analysis.

In March 2005, with some behind-the-scenes help from the British Treasury Department and from the UK government's Department for International Development, the Group of Seven appeared to relent and wrote a joint letter to the World Bank and the IMF asking for an assessment of Nigeria's fiscal sustainability on the basis of the World Bank–IMF Low-Income Country (LIC) DSA template. It specifically asked that Nigeria's fiscal sustainability be viewed "against the broader question of economic sustainability, including its development needs."[9]

Since the Group of Seven finance ministers had asked for a response by April 4 in their March letter, the World Bank and IMF teams decided to divide up the work. IMF staff carried out a base-case DSA by using the LIC DSA template. This did not factor in the incremental fiscal costs needed to meet the MDGs by 2015, but it included all the special modifications dictated by the presence of oil revenues.[10] With oil accounting for 80 percent of government revenues and 90 percent of exports, this finding—not surprisingly—was highly sensitive to changes in the path of oil prices. Any oil-price decline greater than US$4 per barrel would derail public and external debt sustainability.[11]

The World Bank study built on the IMF's baseline. The structure of this study is shown in figure A6.3. The first set of inputs pertained to estimating oil revenues, the second to Nigeria's fiscal and development objectives. These included the importance of strengthening Nigeria's creditworthiness by reducing its high public debt levels of around 72 percent of GDP at the end of 2004.[12] The simulations included an estimate of the fiscal costs of meeting Nigeria's MDGs by 2015, which would raise the non-oil primary deficit above that in the IMF's baseline. The crucial question was whether the high oil-price trajectory in conjunction with the Oil Price-based Fiscal Rule (transferring oil revenues to the budget at a reference price of US$25 per barrel in 2002 prices) would permit Nigeria to both meet the MDGs and reduce its indebtedness. To answer this question, the DSA template was augmented with constraints specifying acceptable thresholds for Nigeria as follows:

• external public debt to be lowered to a maximum 30 percent of GDP

• domestic public debt to be lowered to a maximum of 30 percent of GDP

• a "reserves cushion" of 20 percent of GDP, beginning in 2004 (the base year for the DSA), to be built up to insure against adverse terms-of-trade shocks.

While the 30 percent ceiling for external debt came from the joint World Bank–IMF Debt Sustainability Framework for low-income countries, the 30 percent ceiling for domestic debt would have led to a total public debt ceiling of 60 percent of GDP, reminiscent of the Maastricht criterion for the much richer and more stable euro-zone countries. The need for the reserves cushion came from noting that Nigeria was and remains highly vulnerable to oil-price declines, which could derail its MDG efforts; countries like India and Korea, whose economies are considerably more diversified, were at the time holding reserves of around 30 percent of GDP.

Using this framework, the World Bank study attempted to answer the following question: With high oil prices, if Nigeria committed itself to maintaining a "reasonable" public (domestic plus external) debt to GDP ratio of 60 percent, a prudent level of reserves, and increasing spending to achieve its MDG goals by 2015, would its public-finance position be tenable? In terms of figure A6.3, Nigeria's policy dilemma was between saving (reducing indebtedness and building up reserves) and spending (increasing the non-oil fiscal deficit to develop local infrastructure and increase social-sector outlays in pursuit of the MDGs).

The findings showed that even with the relatively high oil price that then prevailed it would have been impossible for Nigeria to meet the MDGs while also reducing indebtedness and building up reserves. If Nigeria attempted to do all three, as prudence required, it would encounter a sizable solvency problem. A financing gap would emerge by 2012 and would grow rapidly thereafter. The net present value (NPV) of this gap would amount to US$50 billion, implying that even if all of Nigeria's Paris and non–Paris Club debt of US$36 billion at the end of 2004 were to be written off Nigeria would still face a fiscal NPV gap of US$14 billion. The results further showed that under less optimistic scenarios of falling oil prices the fiscal gap would appear much earlier (in 2008), and the gap would climb much higher than US$50 billion (Pinto 2006).

The World Bank and IMF studies were sent to the Group of Seven on time and eventually found their way to members of the Group of Eight and the Paris Club. We were able to use them to demonstrate that Nigeria would need Paris Club debt relief if it was expected to make any appreciable progress toward meeting the MDGs.[13] This was really "outside the box" thinking about debt relief.

Additional Factors Leading to Debt Relief

Finding solutions to the formal Paris Club requirements was a necessary but not sufficient condition for debt relief. Other factors contributed, such as the roles played by civil society, academics, and think tanks in the debate on debt relief and poverty reduction, as well as the lobbying of Paris Club officials of various levels. In addition, the Nigerian legislature played an important role, and other personal contacts in major Paris Club country treasuries were often helpful.

Civil Society, Academics, and Think Tanks

Civil society played an important role in Nigeria's debt relief in both direct and indirect ways. The most powerful role was indirect. Civil society prepared the political ground for greater receptivity to Nigeria's request for relief. The Jubilee 2000 debt-relief campaign had been very helpful. The movement helped bring about the HIPC initiative, which led to the cancellation of poor countries' bilateral debt, and eventually multilateral debt, to the tune of US$41.9 billion (net present values) for some 30 countries—most of them in sub-Saharan Africa. Nigeria had all the characteristics of a HIPC country and had been listed as one initially and then removed from the list. "Nigeria needs debt cancellation," Jeffrey Sachs had argued in 2003. "Its status is comparable to the rest of the HIPC countries and it was once on the list and deserves to be on the list now."[14] Successful debt relief for the HIPCs was helpful to Nigeria's case.

The Make Poverty History campaign was similarly helpful in focusing politicians' attention on the issues hindering developing countries, from making progress on poverty reduction to tackling unsustainable debt burdens and also addressing the inequity and injustice of the global equation in this regard. High-profile campaigners such as Bono and Bob Geldof, as well as the rank-and-file campaigners of Jubilee 2000 and Make Poverty History, exerted pressure that made a difference.

Toward the end of 2004, in the middle of our campaign, the Director-General of the Debt Management Office (Mansur Muhtar) and I realized that getting more direct support and forging partnerships with both domestic and international civil society would be helpful to Nigeria's quest. Mansur found a perfect partner in the person of the former Jubilee 2000 lead campaigner, Ann Pettifor. She worked with us to make the Nigerian story compelling for international non-governmental organizations so they could get beyond Nigeria's unfavorable image abroad and understand the real issues behind the country's quest for debt relief. A website was developed. Pettifor believed that Nigeria was often misunderstood and was a truly deserving country. Her efforts were fruitful in engaging NGOs in Europe and the UK in getting their politicians to notice. Pettifor also helped link Nigerian NGOs interested in the debt-relief campaign to their counterparts abroad. The media in Nigeria and abroad were also contacted to understand the story so that they could report as accurately as possible with the correct facts and figures. Mansur and his team were instrumental in making this happen.

In addition, a wide array of academics, staff members of think tanks, and individual practitioners believed in Nigeria's quest for debt relief and contributed in many ways. They enabled the Economic Team to address important audiences or individuals, and they undertook supportive analyses. One think tank stands out in having made a difference. The Center for Global Development, and particularly Nancy Birdsall and Todd Moss, took an early interest in Nigeria's case and contributed to the IDA analysis discussed above. They also proposed the idea that helped break the impasse in our quest for debt relief: they suggested that Nigeria include an option of buying back a portion of the debt as part of the debt-relief package so that creditor countries would be assuaged. The Center for Global Development was instrumental not only in its intellectual contribution to finding solutions that helped make debt relief happen but also in its advocacy role in the United States and in other development circles.

An influential publication that helped create an atmosphere conducive to debt relief was the report of UK Prime Minister Tony Blair's Commission for Africa, which made a compelling case for debt relief and the need to provide additional development financing for sub-Saharan African countries. The entire push by the UK (the 2005 chair of the Group of Eight) for a "Year of Africa" before the Gleneagles summit was very helpful.

The important part played by civil society in Nigeria's successful quest for debt relief underscores how useful it can sometimes be to develop constructive partnerships between governments and civil-society organizations to find solutions to difficult issues.

The Political Case for Debt Relief

Debt is at once an economic and a supremely political issue, and so is debt relief. In the past, creditor countries of the Paris Club have granted debt relief because it was politically useful, even though the countries still had to meet Paris Club technical criteria. Poland was granted debt relief after the unraveling of the Soviet Union because it was important to support a country trying to democratize and establish a market-based economy. Côte d'Ivoire, Egypt, and Yugoslavia all received debt relief at some stage because of strong political will by Western creditor countries to support them. There is always a political element to the quest for debt relief.

Nigeria did a lot of lobbying—supported by hard facts—to make the political case for debt relief in addition to the economic one. President Obasanjo lobbied presidents of the Group of Eight and of other creditor countries. He made debt relief a measure of his administration's success, so the lobbying went on for six years during his tenure until the relief was granted. The president's central argument was that Nigeria was a young democracy emerging from years of authoritarian military rule. Africa's largest democracy needed nurturing and support, and debt relief would be one way of granting the country a "democracy dividend."[15] I lobbied at the level of the finance ministers, while trying to make sure that the technical work they would ultimately look at and rely on for decisions was done to a high standard to help justify the case for debt relief. Three anecdotes—one involving the United States, one involving Italy, and one involving the United Kingdom, illustrate how agile one had to be to get the right kind of attention for Nigeria's campaign.

I accompanied President Obasanjo on an official visit to the White House on May 5, 2005. One of our objectives was to gain President George W. Bush's support for debt relief so that a message could in turn go to the US Treasury to be more supportive of our request. Although we had garnered sympathy from the Department of State, the National Security Agency, and other parts of the US government, we were still having a bit of a difficult time with the US Treasury, just as we were with other treasury departments of Paris Club members.

We entered the room to find Secretary of State Colin Powell, National Security Adviser Condoleezza Rice, Assistant Secretary of State for African Affairs Jendayi Frazier, and Special Assistant to the President in the National Security Council Cindy Corville. The three women, particularly Condoleezza Rice and Jendayi Frazier, had been supportive of our quest, and had listened separately to my arguments on debt relief on several occasions. I knew that they must have made this opportunity for engagement with President Bush possible.

President Obasanjo explained our desire for debt relief and presented the tremendous change Nigeria was undergoing in implementing difficult economic reforms. President Bush responded that Nigeria was an oil-rich country and that oil prices were high. Nigeria should be lending money to the United States, not asking for debt relief, he joked. It seemed that our request was about to be brushed aside. I was terrified that we were about to miss a unique opportunity. I broke protocol by jumping in and asking my president's permission to explain this issue further to President Bush. He gave his permission, and I knew I had only a few seconds to make our case.

I made two points. First, although oil prices were high, Nigeria was still a poor, large country with a population of 150 million. As such, given that we earned US$25 billion net from oil in 2004, this amounted only to 46 cents per Nigerian per day. Second, Nigeria's economy would have to depend largely on private-sector investment for growth. Yet such investment would be severely limited if we did not invest in infrastructure. We would need more than US$7 billion a year in our estimate for the next five years for this purpose. That was why we would need debt relief to free up resources for this. These two points seemed to catch President Bush's attention and interest, and he said we should send him a letter outlining the points I had just made. At that point, I knew we had made some kind of breakthrough and that we would get his support.

As I made the rounds of Group of Seven finance ministers to argue the case for debt relief, I noted that there was one minister I had not managed to see: Italy's finance minister, Domenico Siniscalco. Each time I tried, I was told he was too busy to receive me. Finally, at the 2005 World Economic Forum in Davos, Switzerland, I heard he was participating and was attending a session close by. I resolved to waylay him in the corridor and make my case. As he exited from his session surrounded by aides, I darted in between them, grabbed his jacket, and introduced myself and my mission. He promptly agreed to a meeting, and over tea I was able to brief him on the Nigerian situation and get his support.

Another anecdote concerns my first meeting with Gordon Brown (then the UK's Chancellor of the Exchequer), in September 2003 at the World Bank–IMF annual meetings in Dubai. Brown's staff gave me just five minutes to brief him. I decided I would not do the expected thing just yet—that is, ask Brown for his support for Nigeria's quest for debt relief. I was sure that this would make his eyes glaze over. Instead I used the five minutes to brief him on Nigeria's ambitious economic reform program and on its progress, adding that only if we implemented this successfully for a year would I ask for his support. This approach, I believe, helped spark his interest in supporting Nigeria. Overall, my strategy for persuasion focused on our important economic reforms rather than on pleading for debt relief as "good" for Nigeria. This strategy worked.

Our case was helped greatly by the presence of people who knew me and my track record in important positions in treasuries and development ministries in the Group of Eight and other creditor capitals. A former colleague of mine, the former World Bank chief economist Nicholas Stern, had joined the UK Treasury as one of Gordon Brown's senior officials. In Germany, my former boss at the World Bank, Caio Koch-Weser, was the deputy finance minister. In Japan, another former colleague, Kiyoshi Kodera, was Senior Deputy Director General at the Ministry of Finance. At the Paris Club Secretariat, Emmanuel Moulin, former alternate Executive Director for France at the World Bank's Board, was secretary-general. This situation generated an invaluable measure of trust. If I said we would deliver on our commitments, important people believed we would do so. That helped smooth our path to debt relief considerably.

Last but not least, the members of the Nigerian legislature worked to convince members of the legislatures of several creditor countries that Nigeria meant business with its reform program and that they should support it by passing appropriate legislation as needed.

The Nigerian House of Representatives also emphasized the country's inability to repay its debt. On several occasions in 2005, Farouk Lawan, the chair of the House Finance Committee, said "We cannot continue. We must repudiate this debt. We are getting close to saying that we won't pay." After the House passed its repudiation resolution, the Senate was under increased pressure to do the same. A delegation from the National Assembly went abroad to make the case for debt relief by meeting with senior government officials, journalists, the Center for Global Development, leading NGOs, and members of the Nigerian diaspora. The whirlwind tour of National Assembly members in 2005 to make the case for Nigeria's debt relief included visits to the United States, the United Kingdom, Germany, Italy, France, and Japan. In the United States, the delegation met with eleven members of the US House of Representatives and with three senators: Chuck Hagel, Christopher Smith, and Barack Obama.

High-Stakes Negotiations

Before our negotiations with our Paris Club creditors began, we did our homework and laid lots of careful groundwork. Nigeria had resolved to ask for debt relief under Evian terms—that is, the customized case-by-case approach to debt relief agreed to by the Group of Eight heads of state at Evian, France, at the 2004 G8 Summit. It seemed the best approach for a country that did not fit into ongoing large-scale debt-cancellation initiatives such as the HIPC initiative. After Evian, our strategy for obtaining debt relief was to ensure that Nigeria fulfilled all or most of the formal requirements for debt relief and set a good track record before making a real push for debt cancellation.

We also tackled the other enabling factors as we were implementing our reform program. There was no need, I thought, to be sent back repeatedly because one requirement or another had not been properly implemented. The first task was to implement our economic reform program successfully for a period of time, similar to what the IMF would have demanded if it had been running the program. The IMF typically has a standby program for 12 to 18 months; we thus focused on implementing reforms with clear measurable results for at least 15 months before beginning the campaign for debt relief. During this period, the IMF undertook three successful reviews of our program. In essence, we waited until we met virtually all of the criteria for Paris Club debt relief mentioned above. The results of our economic reform program were in. GDP growth had tripled to 6 percent per year. The fiscal rule was in place. Reserves had tripled to more than US$21 billion.

On the basis of the IMF's assessments, we felt we had a case for approaching the Paris Club. Previously, we had received helpful advice—based on lessons learned—that it might be best to have a Group of Eight creditor that would serve as Nigeria's sponsor during discussions about debt relief with internal creditors. This creditor could help to convince fellow G8 members of our case and then help push it at the Paris Club. Like other developing countries that had gone through this process, we chose our largest creditor and ally with strong historical ties: the UK, to whom we owed US$8 billion. Prime Minister Tony Blair, Chancellor (later Prime Minister) Gordon Brown, and Secretary for International Development Hillary Benn gave their support. Chancellor Brown, backed up by Treasury and the Department for International Development team, presented Nigeria's case to the G8

finance ministers at various meetings; but it was at the May 29, 2005
G8 finance ministers' meeting before the Gleneagles G8 official summit
on June 6–8 that he was able to convince his colleagues to consider a
debt-relief package for Nigeria.

The major elements were a 60 percent debt cancellation and a buy-
back component. Chancellor Brown negotiated far into the night on
this occasion, telephoning me from time to time. I, in turn, telephoned
President Obasanjo to discuss the acceptability of the G8 creditors'
position. From an opening offer of less than 50 percent debt relief from
creditors and an opening demand for 75 percent debt relief from
Nigeria, Brown was able to convince the G8 finance ministers to move
to 60 percent.

Once this was agreed to, work began to convince the non-G8
members of the Paris Club to accept the deal.[16] This was not easy. There
was resentment that we had gone first to a subset of creditors while
ignoring others. Feelings had to be assuaged, and we made visits (some
at the ministerial level, some at the presidential level) to all the non-G8
creditor countries to convince them of the merits of the case. These
visits occurred in a whirlwind between the middle and the end of June
2005, shortly after the G8 finance ministers' meeting. We knew we had
to conclude these visits and persuade the non-G8 creditors to accept
terms agreed by G8 finance ministers before the June 29 Paris Club
meeting, where the final decision would be made by the Paris Club on
Nigeria's case. We also had to work hard with the members of the Paris
Club's secretariat to get their support.

Late in 2004, Jean-Pierre Jouyet, then president of the Paris Club,
agreed to a rare meeting at which my team from Nigeria's Debt Management Office would present Nigeria's case for reduced debt service
and eventual debt relief to members of the Club. At the presentation,
I made a case based on the reforms, on our human-development indicators, and on our need to invest to reach the Millennium Development
Goals. The case was compelling and was crucial to our convincing the
Paris Club's members that Nigeria merited debt relief. This made it
easier for us to approach non-G8 members later. The deadline President
Obasanjo had set was that we should have some indication or agreement from the Paris Club before the Gleneagles summit, which was to
be held early in July of 2005. Tension continued as we tried to get an
agreement with the Paris Club.

On June 29, 2005, based on Gordon Brown's successful G8 negotiations on our behalf at its last meeting before the Gleneagles summit,

the Paris Club announced its agreement in principle to grant Nigeria debt relief. Underlying the Club's general statement was an agreement to negotiate debt relief on Nigeria's US$30 billion debt. The three essential elements were a standard Paris Club requirement of payment of arrears owed (in Nigeria's case, US$6 billion), Naples terms treatment (that is, a two-thirds write-off) on the remaining US$24 billion of debt, and a discounted (at 25 percent) buy-back on the remaining US$8 billion after reduction under Naples terms. This would yield another US$2 billion of debt relief, for a total debt-relief package of 60 percent, equal to US$18 billion.

Finalization of the debt-relief package would be contingent on Nigeria's getting its reform program formally approved as a Policy Support Instrument by the IMF Board. Nigeria's Policy Support Instrument was approved by the IMF Board in October of 2005. Negotiations between Nigeria and the Paris Club took place immediately thereafter.

The meeting of the Paris Club began in the afternoon of October 18, 2005 at the Finance Ministry in Paris. Before the negotiations began, I opened the session with a presentation—which I had been working on all night—to the Paris Club creditors and the Club's secretariat. Before presenting our formal request, I focused on the progress that had been made on our economic reform programs and challenges that remained. I fielded questions regarding how the debt reduction would allow Nigeria to move forward in its fight against poverty and achieve the MDGs. I emphasized specific projects in education, health, intensification of immunization, and provision of water resources, among others.

That evening, we began the negotiations, which continued until 6:30 the next morning and resumed just four hours later, despite the obvious exhaustion my team and I were feeling. We were given just enough time to return to our hotels for a shower, a change of clothes, and a quick strategy session with our authorities at home before we had to return to the negotiating table.

Despite all my years at the World Bank, I had never realized that one is held hostage at Paris Club negotiation sessions until agreement is reached between the negotiating country and the Paris Club Secretariat on behalf of Paris Club members. The agreed terms of the debt deal are then shared with representatives of member countries and with observer organizations such as the IMF and the World Bank, all of whom are also sequestered in a hall as long as the negotiations last. Once the agreement is blessed by all participants, the deal is sealed.

We did our best to allay the Paris Club members' fears about the sustainability of Nigeria's reforms and about Nigeria's ability to make early payments. The stakes were high, and Nigeria's financial future rested on the outcome. The negotiations were long and tense, and I do not wish that for Nigeria ever again. After reaching agreement on all elements of the package, including the fine print, we signed the momentous Agreed Minute at 4 a.m. on October 20, about 36 hours after the negotiations began.

Debt relief was implemented in three stages between October 2005 and March 2006. Nigeria's external debt burden fell from US$35 billion to approximately US$5 billion. In March of 2006, Nigeria made its final payment to the Paris Club. Nigeria's debt-relief package was the second-largest ever for any country in the Paris Club's fifty-year history, and Nigeria was the first low-income country to be allowed to execute a discounted buy-back on a portion of its debt.

Conclusion: Moving Beyond Debt Relief

The debt-relief package finally obtained was not without controversy. Some civil-society groups and some members of the Nigerian public felt that the country should not have paid anything at all to the Paris Club and should have had a complete write-off. For practical purposes, this was an approach that members of the Club were unwilling to entertain. In the end, the majority of Nigerians accepted the package as good for the country under the prevailing circumstances. Civil-society organizations, both domestic and foreign, were essential partners, and they worked both directly and indirectly to facilitate debt relief.

Debt relief opened hitherto closed doors for Nigeria on the investment front. The country was able to obtain its first-ever sovereign credit ratings from Fitch and from Standard & Poor's. Each of those agencies assigned Nigeria a BB– rating with a stable outlook. This has facilitated greater foreign direct investment flows into the country; flows into the non-oil sector almost doubled from about US$2 billion before debt relief to just under US$4 billion. The beneficial effects of debt relief on the economy have proved sustainable.

I will conclude this chapter by addressing the paradox that "Nigeria obtained major debt relief when oil prices were very high instead of when they were low early in President Obasanjo's first term."[17] Quite apart from the volatility of oil prices and therefore the inadvisability of basing any decision (and especially one as central to the economy as debt relief) on the prevailing oil price, the World Bank study conclusively showed that Nigeria would run into a serious solvency problem if it attempted to meet the Millennium Development Goals while trying to reduce indebtedness and build up reserves, even if oil prices remained high.

But there is more to resolving this paradox. High prices were necessary for Nigeria to address its debt overhang and its reputation overhang. To resolve its debt overhang, Nigeria needed money to buy back its Paris Club debt at a discount. This could happen only if oil prices were sufficiently high, as Nigeria had no other way of raising the needed resources. High oil prices were also necessary for Nigeria to show that it was willing to make a clean break with its past by managing this new windfall well. It needed to assure its creditors that it was not going to squander the proceeds of debt relief. What better way to show this than by managing its high oil revenues successfully?

7 Reflections on the Reforms and Lessons for Reformers

Eight years after the reforms were launched, there is enough distance and sense of perspective to reflect on some fundamental questions: What worked well and what didn't? What could we have done better? What are the lessons learned for the future? I am reflecting on these questions at the very time of another momentous change in my life: my acceptance of the request by President Goodluck Jonathan to resign my job as Managing Director at the World Bank in Washington and return to Nigeria to lead a second round of reforms. If I am to do this again, it must be on the basis of learning from experience to guide the way forward.

My reflections come in the form of a series of questions to myself: Did we diagnose and correctly understand the issues facing the economy? Did we pursue the right reforms? Did we formulate and implement these reforms appropriately? Did we organize adequately to execute the reforms?

Reflections on the Reforms

The best way to answer these questions is to look at the evidence of what happened with the economy and society during the reforms of 2003–2007. As captured in the preceding chapters, implementation of the reforms led to many successes, including the achievement of key outputs and outcomes outlined in the medium-term NEEDS strategy and its precursors.

Accomplishments

Managing Public Finances Better We were successful in improving the management of public finances, curbing volatility by de-linking the oil price used to formulate the budget from the very volatile international oil price. We introduced transparency into public finances by publishing the budget and monthly revenues for all tiers of government, to the delight and appreciation of all Nigerians—except a few corrupt members of the elite. Through openness and tighter fiscal management, we stabilized the macro economy, lowered inflation, and more than doubled economic growth (relative to the average of the previous decade) to 6–7 percent per year. For the first time in the history of Nigerian economic management, we built savings for a rainy day through the operation of the Excess Crude Account (ECA), which accumulated up to US$17 billion, boosting foreign-exchange reserves to US$60 billion as Nigeria entered the Great Recession of the global economy in September 2008. The availability of these savings allowed Nigeria to introduce a fiscal stimulus to the economy equivalent to 0.5 percent of GDP at the height of the global financial crisis, when oil prices fell to below US$40 a barrel from highs of US$146 a barrel just a few months earlier. The savings were deployed to shore up the economy, just as intended.

Launching Structural Reforms We broke the back of several seemingly intractable problems in different sectors by deregulating and liberalizing the telecommunications sector, phasing out the US$1 billion petroleum subsidies, commercializing or privatizing many loss-making enterprises, and concessioning ports and other facilities to the private sector. We began to overhaul and strengthen the civil service. We implemented reforms to strengthen and consolidate the banking and insurance sectors, improving the outlook and performance of the Nigerian financial sector.

Improving Governance, Fighting Corruption, and Strengthening Institutions Nigerians saw blows dealt to impunity among the ruling members of the elite, several of whom, for the first time, were investigated, arrested, convicted, and sent to jail by the Economic and Financial Crimes Commission (EFCC) under Nuhu Ribadu. Institutions were built to help improve governance and fight corruption. The EFCC was one such institution; the Independent Corrupt Practices Committee (ICPC) was another. The Bureau for Public Procurement (BPP), by introducing local and international competitive bidding and value-for-money auditing of public contracts, saved the treasury billions of naira that would have been lost in bloated contracts. Increased transparency in public finances was a strong element in the anti-corruption fight, as it let the public know what monies were coming into the public coffers and enabled them to ask questions of public officials, thus improving accountability. Recovery of stolen assets from Switzerland amounting to US$505 million was another great success appreciated by the public and by civil-society organizations. It forcefully demonstrated to those intent on stealing and exporting public resources abroad that impunity was no longer going to be the norm.

Obtaining Debt Relief The brave attempts at reform and the successes recorded provided the basis for the highly successful Paris Club debt deal accorded to Nigeria in 2005–06. There could be no greater testament to the validity and success of the reforms than the debt deal. The comprehensive debt accord that wiped out US$30 billion of Nigeria's external debt with an outright cancellation of US$18 billion was the second-largest debt deal ever in the history of the Paris Club. A recent evaluation of the deal (Governments of the Netherlands and Belgium 2011) concludes that it was beneficial for Nigeria and for the donors. According to that report, "the combination of policy reforms and the elimination of the debt overhang led to improved creditworthiness and the debt agreement itself acted as a signal that policies had improved and this further improved investor confidence," and "as a consequence there was an increase in foreign direct investment and portfolio flows" (ibid., p. 53). The report concludes that the debt deal had a positive effect on growth and that it reduced poverty.

The logical conclusion to be drawn from the evidence on the beneficial effects of the reforms is that we understood and correctly diagnosed Nigeria's problems. We also appropriately identified the needed reforms. However, there were many things we could have done better with regard to the implementation of the reforms. There was also a lot of unfinished business, especially on the structural reforms. And we could certainly have organized better on implementation. One important point is that we did not focus on the politics and political economy of the reforms as intently as we should have. Let me comment on each of these points.

Implementation of Reforms
Two things illustrate what we could have done better.

Failure to Further Lock In Some of the Reforms Legally The institution of the Oil Price-based Fiscal Rule (OPFR) and the attendant creation of the Excess Crude Account (ECA) are regarded as two of the greatest benefits of the macroeconomic reforms. However, the ECA was controversial. The state governors argued that it was unconstitutional because it prevented the sharing of all revenues among the three tiers of government, as mandated by the constitution. So much energy was expended protecting the revenues in the ECA and fighting the governors on this issue (with President Obasanjo doing battle, sometimes with strong-arm tactics) that it was difficult to focus on other means for securing the ECA. As a result, the ECA was raided several times after the Obasanjo administration ended—even when the triggers for sharing were not met. Resources were transferred to the governors as a form of political appeasement. It was left to two of my successors, Ministers Shamsudeen Usman and Segun Aganga, to create a Sovereign Wealth Fund (SWF) through an act of the National Assembly, with the objective of legally protecting the ECA resources. I implemented the provisions of the Nigerian Sovereign Investment Act (NSIA) on my second tour of duty as Minister of Finance and operationalized the Sovereign Wealth Fund.

It was not that we weren't conscious of the need for legal underpinnings to the reforms. We had worked on the very important Fiscal Responsibility Bill and had gotten it passed. The bill locked in the OPFR; it also set out a transparent and accountable budget framework for the Federal Government and the states—though this was weakened by the states after the Obasanjo administration. It was just that we were engaged in battle on so many fronts, so we missed opportunities to lock in some much-needed reforms. There was also the issue of buy-in and ownership by the states. We probably could have worked harder to get the support for critical reforms.

Inadequate Focus on Job Creation and the Real Sectors of the Economy As a reform team, we were very intent on accelerating economic growth as a means of creating wealth, improving living standards, and reducing poverty. We thus looked at what sectors could be sources of growth. Among the sectors we looked at were agriculture, solid minerals, manufacturing, real estate, and construction. And we did grow the economy. In fact, some the sectors (e.g., agriculture) grew faster than overall GDP. However, we did not focus on metrics for job creation and other impacts on the real sectors, so we had no way of gauging whether the growth created jobs or whether we were experiencing jobless growth. In an environment of high unemployment and underemployment, especially of young people, being able to demonstrate job creation would have been an important means of further convincing Nigerians that the reforms were beneficial.

Unfinished Business

Implementing the structural reforms was tough and required time. Many reforms were left unfinished, and some suffered repeated reversals. The problem was that among these reforms there were clear winners and losers. We did not always focus on cultivating the winners—often the Nigerian public—and use their power to counter the losers. So several privatizations, including those of NITEL and MTEL, were reversed, sometimes because the winning bidder did not perform but sometimes because workers in the entity, losing bidders, and other vested interests (such as parasitic board members) often connived to undermine privatization or commercialization.

In the case of civil-service reform, both the Head of Service (who initially felt he was being undermined, as indeed he probably was) and the majority of civil servants opposed the reforms. The Nigerian public, through a more efficient civil service, would be the winners, but we did not succeed in persuading civil servants or in getting public sympathy and understanding to support the reforms. While the exercise to get rid of "ghost workers" won support, the streamlining of pilot ministries and consequent redundancies of staff did not get as much sympathy or support, because people argued that every civil servant, like most working Nigerians, was likely to be supporting a large number of relatives.

Customs reform was an outright failure. The reason for the failure was opposition from powerful losers in the political elite and in the Customs Service itself who did not want lucrative means of enrichment blocked. Again, we were not able to galvanize the support of potential winners such as members of the business community, traders, and the Nigerian public to push this reform. It was a huge surprise to me that businesspeople who complained about a hugely inefficient and corrupt Customs Service were not willing to be seen as coming out publicly against the Customs Service unless we could guarantee that the reforms would indeed be pushed through. In their eyes, the risks in terms of potential victimization should this fail were too large. In retrospect, they were right, because the proposed reforms did not get the president's political backing.

In addition, structural reforms were unfinished business because they take time. We underestimated how much time it would take to embed and implement the reforms. Completing many reforms in many areas in a four-year administration was probably an unrealistic expectation. Efforts should have been made by the administration to tighten public support for continued implementation of these reforms so that the work would continue to a logical end under any administration.

Politics and Political Economy of Reforms

It was clear to me from the outset of the reform process and the formation of the Economic Team that President Obasanjo saw the team as technocratic and wanted to keep it that way. He also had political advisers, and he was politically adroit himself. He wished for this team to focus on economic issues. Initially, we also clearly saw ourselves in this light. We would keep away from politics, since in any case most of the politicians left a lot to be desired. In fact, I could sense that the politicians felt our team did not appreciate them and regarded them with disdain.

Several incidents between politicians and members of the Economic Team solidified that impression. The best-known and most public incident was the disagreement between Nasir El Rufai and Deputy Senate President Ibrahim Mantu over allegations leaked in the press that Mr. Mantu had asked Nasir El Rufai for bribes to facilitate his confirmation as a minister by the Senate. Mr. Mantu denied this, El Rufai insisted it was true, and the episode almost turned into an affair between the Senate and El Rufai. The incident was eventually handled and calmed by the vice president and the president, but it did not endear the team to the politicians.

As the reforms moved along, the idea that economics could be separated from politics and that the reform team could remain as technocratic as it was became increasingly untenable. We needed to explain NEEDS and the economic reforms to the lawmakers so they could understand and back the reforms. This led to several interactions with politicians and with the main political party, the People's Democratic Party. I found it necessary to get to know the chairs and members of the Appropriations and Finance Committees in the House and the Senate. I had to explain the budget and other finance and economic issues to get their buy-in and support. For the same reason, I also had to interact with the leadership of both houses. Team members had to interact with chairs and members of the committees for areas for which they were responsible. We all learned the political ropes to some extent, and I often felt like a politician in the good sense of the word whenever I had to explain the reform program to legislators or the public. But the political class never really accepted us, and that made it more difficult to implement reform.

We also did not focus on the political economy of the reforms as much as was needed. I have already discussed the inadequacy of our analysis of losers and winners and our failure to persuade winners to back us in some of the most difficult areas.

Another problem was that in Nigeria's very decentralized governance set-up the governors of states controlled almost half of the country's revenues and, according to the constitution, enjoyed considerable autonomy in the use of those resources. They also enjoyed immunity from prosecution, courtesy of the same constitution, and they had very little accountability to anyone. I do not believe that they took the Economic Team seriously at first. But although Nigeria may be made up of 36 states, a Federal Capital Territory, and 774 local governments, it is an integral economic entity, and the constitution does enjoin the Federal Government to manage the economy to the benefit of all Nigerians. Under this provision, we tried to rope the states into better economic management by extending several of the reforms to the state level. The states developed the State Economic Empowerment and Development Strategies (SEEDS), and they were dragged in as participants in the new budgeting approach and its outcome, the Excess Crude Account (ECA). Much of Nigeria's external debt was owed by the states, so they had to keep abreast of the implications of the debt deal. We also tried to persuade them to adopt the more efficient and transparent procurement procedures developed by the Bureau for Public Procurement. Some of them, with our assistance, opened Debt Management Offices and procurement bureaus. The National Planning Office also developed a methodology to rank states according to economic performance and success in poverty reduction. This latter caused an uproar.

Despite these efforts, it is clear that we did not sufficiently understand the importance of the political economy of working with the states, nor did we take all the steps needed to work with the governors. We developed good relationships with a few governors, including those of Cross River, Ogun, Bauchi, Ebonyi, and Kaduna. We visited them in their states, with the hope of using these states as pilots for implementing reforms that could then serve as examples to other states.

But all that was not enough. The involvement of the states in reforms was always difficult to obtain and never sufficiently extensive or deep.

Organizing to Implement the Reforms

The creation of the Economic Team was a huge success, and it remains a landmark for economic management in Nigeria today. It is a tribute to the performance of the team that subsequent administrations also created Economic Teams, though it is debatable whether these successor teams were seen as successful as ours.

But it has to be said that not every aspect of the team's functioning was a success. In the beginning, the team was very cohesive. The core group of about six that did most of the work was even more cohesive than the larger team. Cohesion was built by working together on all aspects of the reforms and building trust. As team leader, I worked very hard at this, making sure that we prepared presentations to various internal and external audiences together and delivered them together. We had the same goals, and we all shared in the credit and success of the team as well as the disappointments.

But as successes occurred, the team began to be seen by others as a powerful club backed by the president—and by politicians and others as something of a threat. The team probably fed this perception by not reaching out sufficiently to other cabinet members who were not on the team. So, just like the state governors, non-team cabinet members felt excluded and did not like or support the team. On the surface at least, they had to support the reform agenda because it was owned by the president. But in those areas where the president lacked political will, as in customs reform, the non-team cabinet members were successful in torpedoing proposals for reforms in cabinet discussions.

In retrospect, we should have worked much harder to carry along the cabinet members who were not part of the team. Toward the end of the administration, the team's cohesiveness began to weaken. Team members began to acquire different agendas and ambitions and to lose focus. That was due in part to a shift in President Obasanjo's focus toward a purely political agenda. (Presidential, gubernatorial, and legislative elections were to be held in early 2007.)

In any event, it was also apparent that, with the achievement of debt relief, the president's greatest "ask" of the team, and in particular of me as its leader, had been achieved. The intense attention and support given to the team was no longer viewed as so necessary or important. My sudden resignation from government in August 2006 certainly did not help matters. It left the team's members upset and reeling, despite the fact that I had been moved to the Ministry of Foreign Affairs three months earlier, and then removed as head of the Economic Team. I resigned because the principles of transparency, openness, and trust that had guided my work in government no longer seemed to obtain and I felt I could not deliver on any important reform agenda in that environment. I suppose that team members felt that, once I had left, the legitimacy and dynamism that I had brought to the team had also diminished or disappeared.

Lessons for Reformers

The above reflections lead me to distill some lessons that I believe are universally applicable to countries undergoing reforms, but may be most relevant in developing countries. I discuss them in no particular order of importance because I believe they are all relevant.

Reforms require a playbook

Reforms should be guided by a vision, a well-thought-out implementation strategy, and a matrix of measurable results. A vision, a strategy, and a well-developed program with expected results constitute a package that can be sold to the public, and also can be used to guide implementation efforts. Because reforms are difficult, it is important to capture the public's attention, imagination, and understanding and (as far as is possible) to get the ruling elite to buy in. Reforms require

Box 7.1
Ten Lessons for Successful Reform

1. Reforms need a playbook.
2. Communication is important.
3. Focus on results and enlist civil society and the public.
4. Build a reform team or an economic team.
5. The political will of the country's leader is important.
6. Look for quick or early wins.
7. Don't open up too many fronts.
8. Pay attention to the politics and political economy of reforms. Analyze winners and losers.
9. Use external restraints and external allies to buttress reforms, but manage this carefully.
10. Manage success.

political will and a social compact. In the Nigerian reform efforts, the NEEDS document played this role.

Communication is important

The public needs to know what reformers are doing and why. Thus, effective communication is necessary. It is best to develop a communication strategy that will focus on outreach to all geographical parts of the country, as well as to the different constituencies for reform. Communication is not a one-off or intermittent affair. It should be continuous, provided there is substance to report about the approach taken, main challenges, and results. This helps to avoid cynicism. Face-to-face contact and explanations by important members involved with reforms are critical.

Focus on results and enlist civil society and the public

Regular communications can be supplemented by a smart media campaign focused on results and the substance and process of reforms. Civil society and the public can be powerful allies in a reform process, generating demand for reform and helping to maintain pressure on politicians to sustain the momentum of reform. They can also be useful in correcting reversals. For example, when monthly publication of government revenues became intermittent after my departure from government, and then stopped after the Obasanjo administration, demand from the public brought it back. By contrast, an uninformed and uneducated civil society can be a dangerous obstacle to reform.

Build a reform team or an economic team

No matter how strong the credentials, one person alone cannot implement reforms. Comprehensive economic reforms are by their nature multifaceted and difficult. Therefore it is important to build a team at the outset to formulate and lead the implementation of the reforms. But putting together a team is not enough. A strong and focused team leader is needed who can engender trust and cohesion in the team. It is important that the team meet regularly—at least once a week—to review the work program and discuss challenges and results. It is also important that each member of the team have a substantial part of the reform program to deliver and to be held accountable for. Ensuring that all members of the team share in its successes and get credit for work done gives them incentives and helps them to maintain momentum. Finally, it is helpful if team members agree on or at least have a meeting of minds on certain principles of operation, such as transparency and personal integrity. This is useful in shielding the team from vested interests and temptations that might undermine its work.

The political will of the country's leader is crucial
Even if a first-rate team is assembled, reform will not occur without the political will and support of the head of state. In fact, there is little point to embarking on reform unless there is a demand for it by the top leadership. Otherwise the going will be tough, with vested interests pushing back. The president, prime minister, or head of government must have the political will to push forward and support reformers making the tough calls. Reformers must continuously assess whether this political will is still evident. If not, they should lock in results already obtained and pull back on the rest. The existence of political will should not be taken for granted. Politics has many twists and turns, and this may change the incentives and agenda of political leaders, especially the head of state, making them less or more enthusiastic to support reforms. Reformers cannot get ahead of the political will to support reforms, though they may be able to galvanize political will for reform.

Look for quick or early wins
Quick and positive results are useful for convincing the public that the reforms are worthwhile and for getting them to buy in to the difficult aspects of reforms. Quick wins can be actions that improve transparency and provide the public with access to information not hitherto available, such as the monthly publication of revenues to all tiers of government that was so popular in Nigeria. Publication of the budget in easily accessible format is also popular. Actions that can tackle corruption can be fairly quick and send a signal of seriousness of intent to the public.

Don't open up too many fronts
It is tempting to pursue a comprehensive approach to reforms. Of course, if the political environment permits, this approach is fine. But comprehensiveness can be problematic if implementation is pursued on too many fronts. This opens the reform effort up to attack on multiple fronts, creates unnecessary noise, and can divert attention from logical pursuit of these reforms as the reformers go on the defensive. Our pursuit of a comprehensive approach in Nigeria, though in retrospect largely appropriate, did lead to some dysfunction of this sort.

With all the firefighting we had to do, we sometimes failed to focus adequately on legally locking in some of the reforms, as was needed.

Pay attention to the politics and the political economy of reforms, and analyze winners and losers

In reform, economics is politics, and the idea that the two can be kept separate is untenable. Thus, it is important that reformers have a plan or a strategy for engaging politicians and lawmakers in the rationale for reforms and getting them to buy in early. This is also important because many reforms must be underpinned and locked in by legislation to prevent reversals. It is also important to engage civil society and the public so as to foster understanding of the reforms so they can support reform-minded lawmakers and hold the government accountable.

Regarding the political economy of reforms, it is crucial to analyze and understand winners and losers so that one can either engage with or protect against them. Winners, if appropriately mobilized, can be powerful allies in preventing losers from undermining reforms.

Incentives or disincentives can be important in turning losers around. For example, if we had been able to convince state governors that their share of the savings from the ECA could be invested so as to bring greater returns to their state treasuries, that might have diminished if not completely removed their opposition to accumulating those savings. Similarly, a less permissive Nigerian constitution that didn't give blanket immunity to governors while in office would have served as a check on mismanagement of public resources and allowed for more accountability on their part.

Use external restraints and external allies to buttress reforms, but manage this carefully

External restraints can be powerful tools to provide a rationale for reforms. But there must be a careful balance so that the reform agenda is not seen as externally driven. For example, regional or international trade agreements can provide the impetus to reform a country's trade regime. In Nigeria, the tariff regime is politicized, with different business groups and their political backers interfering in the setting of tariffs or even asking for the implementation of non-tariff barriers to benefit their businesses. To get around this and begin the reform of the country's trade regime, we tied reform proposals to Nigeria's signature and accession to the Economic Community of West African States

(ECOWAS) Common External Tariff (CET). Though Nigeria had signed the agreement, Nigeria was the last country to do so and had never implemented it. We used this to persuade the president to back reforms to rationalize our tariff structure.

The Paris Club debt deal provides another example. Paris Club rules require an IMF agreement to reach a deal. An IMF agreement was politically unacceptable in Nigeria, but if the agreement basically calls for macroeconomic, structural, and governance reforms with quantitative targets and results. By arguing that the reforms were needed to move Nigeria's economy forward in any case, we were able to craft a homegrown reform program around these issues that was at least as tough as what the IMF would have required. We got the IMF to accept our package in September 2005 in the form of the first-ever IMF non-financed program, known as a Policy Support Instrument, and then persuaded the Paris Club to accept this as a valid IMF program. The approach was a fine balancing act in the use of an external restraint in a way acceptable to a domestic audience.

The international community can be a powerful ally to support reforms in a developing country by speaking out or backing reformers. The World Bank and the IMF were helpful in this regard. Jim Wolfensohn, Gordon Brown, Tony Blair, Bill Clinton, George W. Bush, Anne Krueger, Condoleezza Rice, George Soros, and Bono were very helpful in this regard. Again, this has to be managed so the balance of support is right and it does not begin to look to a domestic audience as if the reforms are externally driven. But members of the international community can be fickle and play largely to their own interests, so reformers would be wise not to put too much stock in their goodwill and support.

Manage success
This may sound like a strange lesson, but experience shows that it may be easier to manage failure than to manage success. If reforms fail, reformers either are booted out, back out, or recalibrate and come back with a better approach. Reformers always worry a lot about failure, but they seldom worry about success. Usually success is well rewarded, but success can also have its downside. It may lead to unduly high expectations for reformers on all aspects of the reforms. It may also bring excessive accolades for reformers, either as a group or individually. This can set up jealousies within and outside the reform team that can be cleverly exploited to undermine the team's cohesion and the

implementation of the reforms. In our case, I certainly felt, after the highly successful Paris Club deal, that the ground somehow shifted for the reform team and for me personally. There was a sense among some of the elite groups and advisers to the president that the Economic Team had become too powerful and should be curbed. This led to considerable undermining of the team's cohesion and of its standing with the president. That, together with the political agenda for elections, served to shift the president's attention away from reforms and the reform team.

These lessons are not exhaustive. I am sure others who have implemented reforms may have their own lessons to add. But I believe these lessons can serve as an important guide to reformers, policy makers, and development practitioners setting out on the difficult path of turning around a poorly performing economy or spurring the growth and development of a struggling one.

Let me end on a personal note. Perseverance does pay off. Sticking to principles matters. And virtue can be its own hard-won reward. For me, the reforms were a tough road, but a rewarding one. I won and lost friends along the way, and created trust, but also suffered betrayal. In the final analysis, I learned a lot about my country, and I have absolutely no regrets.

8 Conclusions and a Look Forward

The implementation of reforms in the second Obasanjo administration (2003–2007) broke a cycle of despair and cynicism among Nigerians about the prospects and future of their country. It showed that it is possible to bring about change, that there are Nigerians selfless enough to do this without sinking into corruption or personal gain, and that indeed it is possible to reform this hitherto unreformable country.

But did the reforms launch Nigeria on a path of sustainable growth and development? The jury is still out. Nigeria has certainly been growing at a respectable 7 percent average annual rate since the reforms, but it is clear that the Nigerian economy has not yet fundamentally transformed, is not yet creating the numbers of jobs needed to absorb the youth, and faces a large unfinished reform agenda.

This unfinished agenda has been analyzed by many people (including me),[1] many institutions (including the World Bank and the International Monetary Fund),[2] and by the Nigerian government itself (in a forward-looking report titled "Nigeria Vision 20: 2020"). It is nevertheless important to summarize this agenda in the context of emerging challenges and opportunities in the global climate.

The Global Context

The food, fuel, and financial crises of 2007–08 and their aftermath, the Great Recession, created a climate of global uncertainty from which there has been very slow recovery in global growth. The Greek and Irish debt crises, and similar worries for Portugal, Spain, and Italy, have led to a euro crisis, which in turn has refueled global uncertainty. In conjunction with the debt-ceiling crisis in the United States arising from the protracted political negotiations to raise borrowing limits, and the ensuing downgrade of the United States' credit rating by Standard &

Poors,[3] global capital markets have been spooked, and there are fears of a double-dip recession.

Major events related to climate change in 2010 and 2011 (droughts and floods in important food-producing countries such as China, Pakistan, and Australia), and earthquakes in Japan, New Zealand, Chile, and elsewhere, have exacerbated the uncertainty. Should a double-dip recession occur, Nigeria could again be severely impacted, as it was in the Great Recession, principally through a drop in the global demand and price for its main export, oil. This would have a detrimental effect on Nigeria's growth prospects. Nigeria's great dependence on petroleum products and its vulnerability to global volatility of commodity markets are important factors in the country's need to reshape its economic structure and growth pattern and diversify its economic base.

The global context, while posing challenges, also provides opportunities for Nigeria to tackle its economic problems and diversify. For one thing, capital markets in the developed countries no longer provide the attractive returns they once did. With the surplus savings in these countries, the risk appetite of investors for emerging and frontier markets has increased. Nigeria could and should benefit from this. In addition, in contrast to the slow growth in the developed countries, emerging market countries (China, Brazil, India, and others) are growing at a fast pace, in the range of an average 6–10 percent per year. This has fueled demand in these countries for primary commodities to support their growth as well as new markets for their products and new investment destinations for their capital. South-South foreign direct investment is fast becoming the norm in many developing countries. Nigeria, with a population of 160 million and a dynamic entrepreneurial class, is well positioned to benefit from this trend, which can be a springboard for diversification.

Transforming the Nigerian Economy

To diversify and transform its economy, Nigeria must complete the reform agenda begun in 2003 and go beyond it to focus on the real sectors of the economy as engines of job creation. In completing this agenda, to ensure a greater chance of success, it will be important for reformers to consider the lessons stated in chapter 7. Though the terrain appears as difficult as ever, the potential to truly transform the economy is even greater than in the first reform episode because of the global context. Several areas are crucial.

Creating Jobs

The need to create jobs is the most important problem confronting the Nigerian economy now and for years to come, especially for the increasing numbers of youths entering the job market. Studies show that as much as a quarter of Nigeria's working age population aged 15–65 years is not in the labor force (Treichel 2010, p. 19). Fully 70 percent of Nigeria's 160 million people are 30 years of age or younger, and there is evidence of rising unemployment among youth (Treichel 2010, p. 23). If Nigeria could create the needed number of jobs, it could turn this demographic dividend of a young working-age population into a development dividend. To do this, Nigeria must build a strong economic foundation by focusing on the following four things.

Strengthening the Macroeconomic Framework Since 2007, Nigeria has been fiscally lax, sometimes running deficits in excess of 3 percent of GDP and directing most of these resources to salaries out of other ever-increasing recurrent expenditures (now 74 percent of the federal budget), with little left for capital expenditures. There is a great need to put the fiscal house in order, particularly to increase resources available for investment. In this context, the ever-rising levels of domestic debt, though not yet a threat, should be watched. In addition, in view of the continued dependence on oil, management of volatility through application of the Oil Price-based Fiscal Rule and prudent operation of the new Sovereign Wealth Fund will be important to ensuring fiscal stability and prudence. All this should be accompanied by appropriate monetary and exchange-rate policies conducive to economic diversification.

Improving the Investment Climate Nigeria's rank of 133 out of 183 countries surveyed in the World Bank's Doing Business report 2012 is evidence of how difficult it is to invest and to grow businesses there— the very actions that are needed to create jobs.[4] Nigeria has been slipping in the rankings, going from 120 in 2009 to 133 in the latest survey. On some of the most critical business indicators, Nigeria performs badly. It ranks 180 in registering property, 84 in dealing with construction permits, 149 in trading across borders, 138 in paying taxes, and 116 in starting a business. Nigeria badly needs to pursue reform of its investment climate in order to become more attractive to domestic and foreign investors.

Fighting Corruption   Corruption in Nigeria remains a serious problem, both in perception and in reality. Progress was made during the reform program in improving transparency, in building anti-corruption institutions, and in checking impunity among the corrupt elite. The vast majority of Nigerians are honest and hard-working citizens; only a tiny minority gives the country a bad name. Fighting corruption must remain a centerpiece of efforts to grow and develop Nigeria's economy. At the onset of the second Obasanjo administration, in 2003, when we began the reforms, Nigeria had one of the worst Transparency International (TI) corruption perception index scores, ranking of 132 out of 133 countries assessed.[5] By the end of the reform program, in 2007, Nigeria ranked 147 out of 179 countries assessed. In 2010, Nigeria's score was 2.4, with a ranking of 134 out of 178 countries. Though there has been some improvement by this one measure, Nigeria is still in the wrong neighborhood as far as the rankings are concerned. To make further gains on the anti-corruption front, specific impediments that encourage rent-seeking behavior must be identified and dealt with.

One good way to fight corruption is to work on the investment climate. Reducing requirements for business and property registration and for trade transactions, including improving the Customs Service, will lead to reduced corruption, with measurable effects on business development and job creation.

Improving the transparency of the oil accounts and the transparency of government finances at both federal and state levels are other areas for action. The private sector in Nigeria itself is not immune to corruption. Continued actions to clean up and strengthen the banking sector and sanitize capital markets will be crucial.

Action against impunity must continue. Cynicism about the fight against is greatest when allegations of corrupt acts on the part of the elite are not investigated with any vigor or even investigated at all. That is why it is important to bring credibility to the effort with specific actions and measurable results.

Efforts need to be intensified at the international level to recover the billions of dollars of Nigeria's stolen assets lying in the banks of developed countries. Though there has been progress since 2005, there is still a long way to go. Some developed countries continue to use unhelpful laws and legal procedures to prevent their banks from returning assets. It is unfortunate that developed countries have been aggressive in exerting pressure on perceived tax havens to return the proceeds of their citizens' tax evasion but are not willing to press jurisdictions harboring stolen assets to return those assets to developing countries. Nigeria must make this issue an integral part of its fight against corruption to recover these monies so they can be used to fund poverty-reducing projects, and to send a message of "no impunity" to those who would spirit corruptly acquired assets abroad.

Completing Structural Reforms The unfinished deregulation, liberalization, and privatization agenda for several sectors must be completed. Deregulating the downstream petroleum sector and phasing out of the huge US$13 billion in subsidies to the price of petroleum products should be top priorities. The mechanism for administering the subsidies has proven imperfect and subject to fraud and corruption. The subsidies are poorly targeted and are a burden to the treasury. They benefit the upper classes disproportionately relative to the poor.

Phase-out should be accompanied with a sound safety net program to cushion the impact on poor people and build trust with the population. Education and communication with the public on this issue is paramount. Action by government to fully phase out the subsidy in January 2012 was courageous and the right thing to do but had all the hallmarks of déjà vu in implementation. This is why the experience was particularly painful for me.

Deregulation will also serve as an incentive for private-sector investment in petroleum refining. Nigeria refines only a small fraction of the refined products that it consumes per day. The rest is imported. It is sad that citizens of a country that is a leading exporter of oil and gas often have to queue up to buy gasoline. Passage of a cogent Petroleum Industry Bill will provide the framework needed to guide the development of the industry.

Equally important is completion of ongoing work on unbundling of power-sector assets, their privatization, and liberalization of the sector. This should be accompanied by strengthening of the regulatory framework to protect consumer interests and to maintain a proper balance of interests between electric power consumers and operators.

It will also be important to complete the work on port concessions and focus on needed investments by both government and the private sector to make the ports efficient and cost effective. This should be accompanied by trade and customs reforms. The ports are rife with corruption, and Nigeria is falling behind in the competitiveness of its ports relative to those in neighboring countries. If these reforms are not completed soon, Nigeria will lose an even larger amount of its trade to neighboring countries.

Civil-service reform is another difficult unfinished agenda. More than streamlining is needed. Capacity must be built, and rules that provide no incentives to top performers or to those with specialized skills must be scrapped.

In the financial sector, ongoing work to sanitize and strengthen the banking sector and to restore confidence in capital markets must be completed. Continued attention is critical to building capacity and strengthening financial-sector regulators to enable them to perform their functions properly. Nigeria rarely evaluates or audits programs, processes, or the functioning of institutions. As the country focuses on completing various aspects of the reform agenda, it should establish performance benchmarks for reformed institutions, and should evaluate whether programs are yielding the desired results.

Working on the Real Sectors

Progress can be made on transforming the real sectors of the Nigerian economy to create jobs. It is indicative of Nigeria's potential that, despite the unfinished reform agenda, the economy has recorded robust growth in the last eight years. Now it is important to translate this growth into jobs and to accelerate its momentum.

Infrastructure

Without improvements in infrastructure, Nigeria's economy will not be able to produce the job-creating growth that is needed. In particular, small and medium-size enterprises will not be able to grow, as infrastructure costs and bottlenecks make it difficult for them to be competitive.

The work that needs to be done has been much discussed and is well known. Nigeria's infrastructure deficit is most stark in the power sector. Different governments have tried to address the problem in recent times—not very successfully. The regulatory framework, the tariff

regime for both electricity and gas, physical problems with gas supplies, and privatization of the unbundled power-sector institutions
have stood in the way.

The goals for reforming the power sector should be modest and
creative. They should address the basic service-delivery needs of both
households and businesses. It is far more important to look toward
modest improvements in power generation, transmission, and distribution and seek creative means to achieve these than to promise a
doubling or tripling of the current 4,000-megawatt capacity in the
medium term and not achieve it.

For instance, it is possible to look seriously at alternative energy
sources and off-grid solutions to assist households and small businesses
in rural areas and crowded city slums. It is also possible to consider dedicated power supply to concentrated economic zones where enterprises
can cluster. Nigeria requires an estimated US$10 billion per year for
infrastructure investments, including power-sector investments, in the
next decade. Though not an insurmountable obstacle, that will require
financial creativity to leverage private-sector and multilateral resources
to complement government investment, especially when there is visible
competition with other emerging market and developing countries
for infrastructure investment. Interim solutions and results will therefore be important to assuage the expectations of the population.

But power is not the only aspect of infrastructure that requires work.
Roads, highways, rail, ports, and information and communications
technology also require attention. Some of Nigeria's main transport
arteries—such as the Lagos-Ontisha, Lagos-Ibadan, Abuja-Benin, and
Kano-Lagos highways—have become so clogged that they are now
death traps. There is no reason why these cannot be made into self-
sustaining toll highways through public-private partnerships. Nigeria
will need all the avenues of support available, together with some
financial engineering, to fund all its needed infrastructure investments
over the next decade. Mobilizing these resources and investing them
efficiently will be a major challenges.

Agriculture

Nigeria boasts several sectors that can be sources of growth and can
thus provide a solution to the diversification challenge. These are the
sectors to focus on for the future. Nigeria's large domestic market and
potential for export make the development of these sectors an attain-
able objective. First and foremost is agriculture, which accounts for 40

percent of GDP—the largest of all sectors. With growth at a rate of 6 percent per year since 2009, and even faster before then, this sector has been one of the fastest-growing of the non-oil sectors of the economy. Nigeria has the capacity to feed itself, yet expenditures on food imports total about US$10 billion a year.

The objectives of sectoral transformation should be food security and development for export of value chains in which Nigeria has a comparative advantage. The focus on food security is important in light of recurring global food-price crises and the uncertainties associated with of climate change. It is difficult to imagine future sectoral development in the absence of adaptation to the emerging climate uncertainties.

According to Treichel (2010, p. 20), agriculture is at the center of an interesting structural change in the Nigerian labor force—a change that entails a shift from wage employment toward agricultural employment. The share of the labor force in family agriculture rose from 30.8 percent in 1999 to 37.8 percent in 2006 as job creation in the formal sector stagnated. Nigerian agriculture is experiencing the reverse of what is normally observed in other countries—a shift of labor from agriculture to other sectors as the economy is developing. This can help boost productivity in agriculture. Indeed, the growth observed in Nigerian agriculture is not due to productivity increases, but to exploitation of additional land.

Thus, there is potential for development of the sector through productivity gains and for development of additional land through attention to smallholder farmers as well as larger commercial agriculture. The key will be improving the policy environment for the sector—for example, reforming the inefficient fertilizer subsidy regime to benefit more small farmers—and modernizing it by implementing a value-chain approach that supports farmers from farm to market. Several important value chains have been identified for development (see Treichel 2010 and Adesina 2011): meat and poultry, dairy, rice, oil palm, cotton, cocoa, sorghum, and cassava.

Nigeria will revive the Abuja commodity exchange to provide an electronic platform for trading agricultural products. With the attendant investments in warehouses, and potential for farmers to use warehouse receipts as collateral for loans, this could help revolutionize farmers' ability to invest in and pursue a modernized agriculture.

Manufacturing

Nigeria's manufacturing sector has been in decline, hit hard by deficiencies in infrastructure (particularly the power deficit), unfair competition from smuggled manufactured products, and a lack of investment in modern equipment. Whole subsectors, such as textiles and tires, have been particularly hurt, and capacity utilization is low.

But Nigeria has the potential to revive once the above problems are tackled creatively. There is the potential to provide infrastructure for new entrants in a more affordable fashion by clustering enterprises in an industrial zone or a free-trade zone. The trade and tariff regime can certainly be reformed in a manner that encourages and supports the manufacturing sector. Nigeria's large domestic market and its dominance of the Economic Community of West African States (ECOWAS) market could attract investment from emerging market countries like China, whose unit costs of production for labor-intensive manufacturing is rising. As those countries move up the manufacturing value chain, countries like Nigeria can benefit as alternative investment destinations for labor-intensive goods. Nigeria should therefore position itself to take advantage of these possibilities.

Construction and Housing

There is considerable potential for the construction and housing sector to drive growth, create jobs, and contribute to a diversification of the economy. Nigeria has a housing deficit of 12–16 million units. An additional 720,000 units are needed per year. Since Nigeria has one of the fastest urbanization rates in sub-Saharan Africa, the housing deficit can be a real driver for economic growth. The main obstacles confronting this sector are the lack of a mortgage finance system and bureaucratic obstacles to the registration of land and property. Under the 2003–2007 reform program, we began to lay the foundations for the development of a mortgage market, but that effort was truncated. It will have to be revived as the basis for launching this sector.

Services

In the services sector, the potential for the entertainment industry to create value and create jobs has now been proven. Nollywood has become the third-largest film industry in the world by value (US$ 250 million per year) after Hollywood and Bollywood. On average it churns out 40 movies per week. It provides direct employment to an estimated

200,000 people, with another million jobs indirectly linked to this (Treichel 2010, p. 28). Yet the industry has hardly reached its potential. Quality and intellectual-property rights are problematic, as is access to financing. The production and marketing chains need to be organized more tightly. Nollywood has been entirely driven by the private sector and is a good illustration of what can happen when the government stays out of the way. It would be helpful to enhance industry access to finance, including for steps to improve quality, and to tighten the enforcement of intellectual-property rights.

Nigeria also should focus on information and communication technologies (ICT), both from the infrastructure side (to spur development of other sectors) and as a subsector in itself capable of generating outsourcing and other types of jobs linked to technology. Kenya—with its payments systems linked to mobile phones, and development of applications for crowd sourcing, such that created by the Ushahidi Group—provides an example of how ICT is spurring the creative energies of the youth and creating jobs.

Other Sectors
The highlighting of the above sectors does not mean that they form an exhaustive list of sectors upon which to focus as sources of growth and diversification for the Nigerian economy. For instance, Nigeria has about 34 solid minerals, including tantalite, bitumen, gold, zinc, and granite, in commercially exploitable quantities; there is potential to channel investment and create jobs in this sector. And of course continued investment in the mainstay oil and gas sector will be necessary to maintain the revenue base of the economy as it diversifies.

Human Development
Finally, the transformation of Nigeria's economy cannot take place without adequate attention to this transformation's implications for human development. Nigeria will need the skills base to carry forward this transformation, and it will need a healthy population. Nigeria has some of the worst human-development indicators in the world and is not on track to meet most of the health and education Millennium Development Goals. This means that its failing education and health sectors should be reformed to better serve households and businesses. As I have said elsewhere (Okonjo-Iweala 2010), it is in the interest of the business sector to open up a dialogue with educators on the need for skills, especially at the technical, vocational, and tertiary levels.

There are good examples from East Asia, such as Korea, of how this can work to the benefit of an entire economy.

The agenda for Nigeria's transformation is long, but it is also clear and exciting. Getting Nigeria on a sustainable development path is not just important for Nigeria; it is critical for West Africa (Nigeria contributes two-thirds of the subregion's GDP) and for sub-Saharan Africa (Nigerians constitute one-fourth of Africa's population). When Nigeria succeeds in transforming itself, it will transform Africa, and the vision of Africa as a fast-growing emerging economic group of nations, comparable to the BRIC countries, will become a reality.

Appendix: Figures and Tables

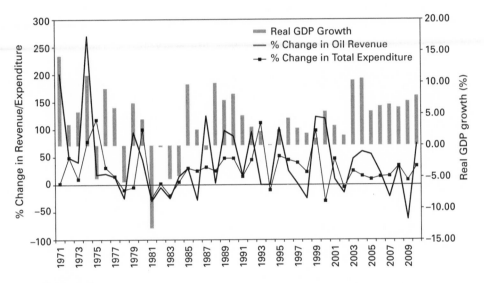

Figure A2.1
A dangerous pattern: government oil revenues, expenditures, and GDP growth, 1971–2010. Sources: Federal Government of Nigeria staff estimates (2011) and author's calculations.

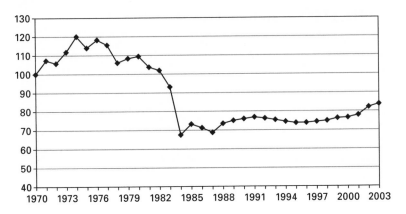

Figure A2.2
Real non-oil GDP per capita, 1970–2005 (1970 = 100). Source: Budina, Pang, and van Wijnbergen 2007.

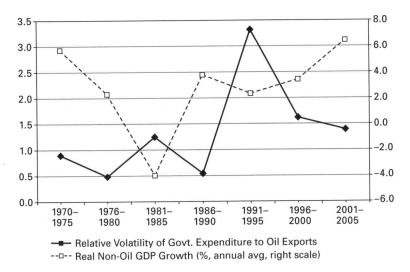

Figure A2.3
The cost of volatility, 1970–2005. Source: Budina, Pang, and van Wijnbergen 2007.

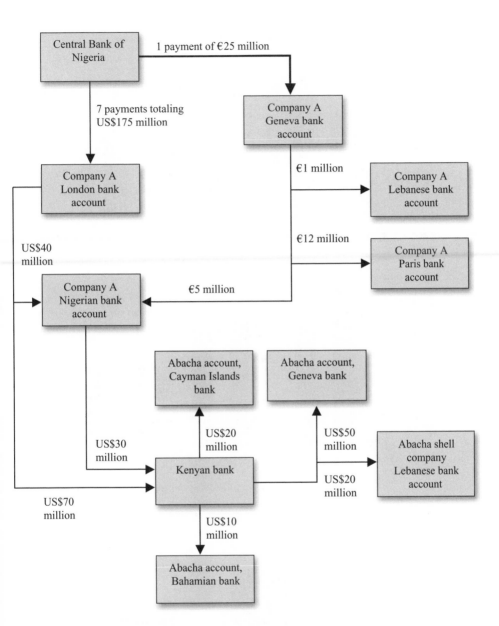

Figure A5.1
Following the money: how payments from the Central Bank of Nigeria to Multinational Company A were laundered to accounts in Abacha in 1998. Adapted from page 4 of Okonjo-Iweala 2007a.

(a)
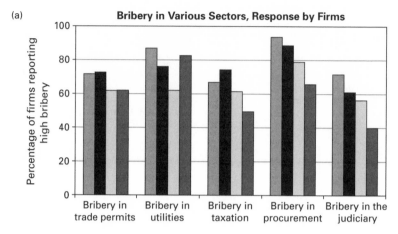

(b)
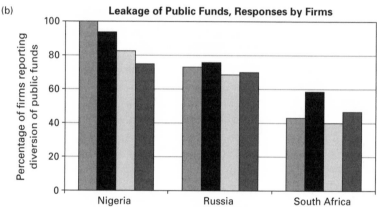

(c)
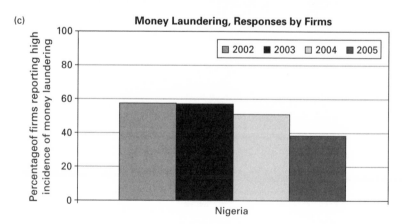

Figure A5.2
Curbing corruption in Nigeria, 2002–2005 (responses by Nigerian firms). Source: Kaufmann 2005.

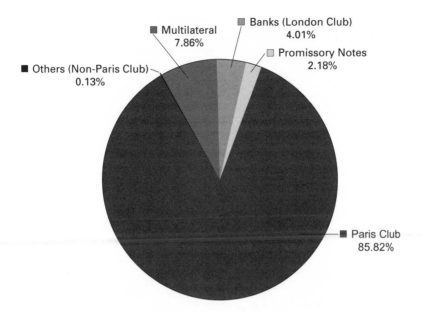

Figure A6.1
Nigeria's external debt, by creditor, year-end 2004. Source: Paris Club.

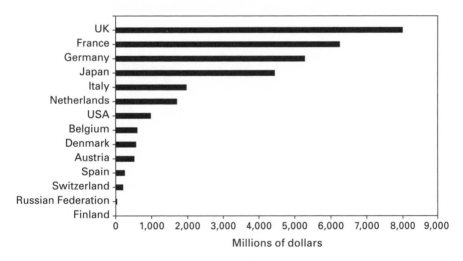

Figure A6.2
Nigeria's debt to Paris Club countries, year-end 2004. Source: Paris Club.

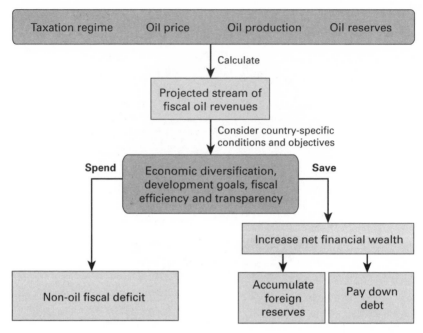

Figure A6.3
The World Bank's Debt Sustainability Analysis for Nigeria. Source: World Bank 2005.

Table A1.1
Members of Nigeria's Presidential Economic Team.

Early members	
Dr. Ngozi Okonjo-Iweala	Minister of Finance (Chair)
Mrs. Nenadi E. Usman	Minister of State—Finance
Mallam Nasir El-Rufai	Minister of the Federal Capital Territory
Mrs. Oby Ezekwesili	head of "due process" (later Minister of Minerals, then Minister of Education)
Prof. Charles Soludo	Economic Adviser to President; later Governor of Central Bank of Nigeria
Mr. Bode Agusto	Director-General (Budget)
Mallam Nuhu Ribadu	Head of Economic and Financial Crimes Commission
Mr. Steve Oronsaye	Principal Secretary to President
Engr. Funsho Kupolokun	Group Managing Director, Nigerian National Petroleum Corporation
Dr. Mansur Muhtar	Director-General of Debt Management Office
Ms. Ifueko Omoigui	Chair of Federal Inland Revenue Service
Dr. Joseph Nnanna	Director of Central Bank of Nigeria (stand-in for CBN Governor)
Dr. Bright Okogu	Executive Secretary to Economic Team and Senior Adviser to Minister of Finance

Later additions	
Mrs. Irene Chigbue	Director-General of Bureau for Public Enterprises
Prof. Kunle Wahab	Special Adviser to President of Budget Monitoring and Price Intelligence Unit
Dr. Osita Ogbu	Economic Adviser to President, replaced Charles Soludo
Mr. Kayode Naiyeju	Accountant-General of Federation
Alhaji Ibrahim Dankwambo	Accountant-General (replaced Mr. Naiyeju in 2005)
Mallam Adamu Bello	Minister of Agriculture
Dr. Aliyu Modibbo	Minister of Commerce
Chief Femi Fani-Kayode	Minister of Culture and Tourism
Prof. Leslye Obiora	Minister of Solid Minerals

Table A2.1
Nigeria's volatile macroeconomy: an international comparison, 1961–2000. Source: World Bank 2003.

Variable	Number of countries[a]	Nigeria's rank	Median volatility (percent)	Nigeria's volatility (percent)
Terms of trade[b]	90	3	10	27
Per capita real revenue[c]	71	3	11	41
Real exchange rate[d]	84	4	7	31
Consumer prices	114	21	7	19
Monetary growth	125	32	14	20
Per capita real GDP	87	9	4	8

a. Countries with 15 or more observations during the period. Eighty percent of countries had observations for 20 years or more.
b. Nigeria was third out of 90 countries for the standard deviation of terms of trade in levels from 1960 to 2000.
c. Deflated by the consumer price index. Nigerian data include stabilization account drawings in 1995 and 1999.
d. For 1979–2000, defined so that a movement up is an appreciation.

Table A2.2
Effect of volatility on social outcomes: Nigeria compared with other countries in 2004. Source: World Bank's World Development Indicators database, 2004.

	Nigeria	South Africa	Sub-Saharan Africa	Low-income countries
GNI per capita, Atlas method (current US$)	430	3,670	606.54	507.02
Immunization, measles (percent of children aged 12–23 months)	35	81	64.48	63.45
Improved sanitation facilities, urban (percent of urban population with access)	53	79	53.28	60.56
Improved water source (percent of population with access)	48	88	56.24	75.09
Life expectancy at birth, total (years)	43.65	44.64	46.22	58.75
Mortality rate, infant (per 1,000 live births)	101.4	54	100.47	79.52
Mortality rate, under 5 (per 1,000)	196.6	67	168.19	121.59

Table A2.3

The cost of volatility, 1992–2002 (annual percentage changes). Sources: Federal Government of Nigeria; IMF 2001, 2003, 2005.

	1992	1993	1994	1995	1996	1997	1998	1999	2000	2001	2002	1992–2002 avg.
Total GDP	2.43	0.58	–1.61	2.29	6.20	2.77	0.23	1.49	5.64	3.31	1.42	2.25
Oil GDP	2.27	1.24	0.12	2.17	4.48	1.47	–5.39	–4.13	11.54	1.42	–11.63	0.32
Non-oil GDP	2.52	0.21	–2.58	2.35	7.17	3.51	3.40	4.39	2.84	4.28	7.96	3.28
CPI inflation (year-on-year)	48.8	61.3	76.8	51.6	14.3	10.2	11.9	0.2	14.5	16.5	12.2	28.94

Table A2.4
Nigeria's stabilizing macroeconomy, 2003–2006 (annual percentage changes, unless otherwise specified). Sources: Nigerian authorities and IMF staff estimates and projections; IMF 2006a.

	2003	2004	2005	2006
Real GDP (at 1990 factor cost)	10.9	6.1	7.2	6.1
Non-oil GDP (at 1990 factor cost)	4.4	7.4	8.6	7.0
Consumer price index (period average)	14.0	15.0	17.9	9.4
Consumer price index (end-year)	23.8	10.1	11.6	8.5
Overall fiscal balance[a]	–1.3	7.7	9.9	12.0
Non-oil primary fiscal balance[b]	–34.4	–35.2	–39.8	–39.6
External current account balance[c]	–2.7	4.1	12.1	14.2
Gross external reserves (US$billion)	7.5	17.0	28.3	45.8
In months of imports of goods and services	3.4	6.1	8.8	13.1
Excess crude account balance (US$billion)	—	5.9	10.9	8.3

a. Commitment basis, in percent of GDP.
b. Cash basis, in percent of non-oil GDP.
c. In percent of GDP.

Table A3.1
Liabilities of selected commercially oriented public enterprises to external and internal creditors (billions of naira) as of 2004, with liabilities to the Federal Government of Nigeria and pension liabilities included. Source: presentation by BPE Director-General Irene Chigbue to Nigeria Diaspora Conference, Toronto, 2007.

NigerianRailwayCorporation	18.20
NNMCOku-Iboku	16.80
NigerianFertilizerCompany(NAFCON)Onne	15.00
NisucoBacita	14.70
NPMJebba	12.00
NigerianPortsAuthority	6.60
FSFCKaduna	4.90
NigeriaAirways	3.90
IwopinPulpandPaperCo.	3.40
SteyrNigeriaLtd	2.30
NMTOshogbo	2.00
JosSteelRollingMill	1.30
AnamcoEnugu	1.00
OshogboSteelRollingMill	0.99
NationalIronOreMining	0.71
VolkswagenofNigeria	0.65
ElemePetrochemical	0.63

Table A3.2
Details of gross proceeds and disbursements (table produced by MIT Press from original Bureau of Public Enterprises document).

S/N	Transaction	Method of sale	Name of investor	Gross proceeds '000	Creditors/ staff payments '000	Other expenses '000	Total cost of sales	Net proceeds '000	Remarks
1	Benue Cement Co. Plc	Core Investor Sale	Dangote Industries Limited (Nigeria)	918,316					
		Shares Sale	Individuals	111,317	668,033	89,675	757,708	271,925	
2	Cement Company of Northern Nigeria Plc	Core Investor Sale	Scancem (Norway)	622,761					
		Shares Sale	Individuals	145,087		56,201	56,201	711,647	
3	West African Portland Cement Co. Plc	Core Investor Sale	Bluecircle Industries Limited	1,798,550					
		Shares Sale	Individuals	1,146,158		60,881	60,881	2,883,827	
4	Unipetrol Nigeria Plc	Core Investor Sale	Ocean and Oil Nigeria Limited	1,593,750					
		Shares Sale	Individuals	1,343,390		234,562	234,562	2,702,578	
5	African Petroleum Plc	Core Investor Sale	Sadiq Petroleum Nigeria Limited	2,308,824					
		Shares Sale	Individuals	1,711,620		322,893	322,893	3,697,551	

Table A3.2
(continued)

S/N	Transaction	Method of sale	Name of investor	Gross proceeds	Creditors/staff payments	Other expenses	Total cost of sales	Net proceeds	Remarks
6	National Oil & Chemical Marketing Co. Plc (now CONOIL Plc)	Core Investor Sale	Conpetro Nigeria Limited	7,644,533					
		Shares Sale	Individuals	1,605,523		4,560,740	4,560,740	4,689,316	
7	F S B International Bank Plc	Share Flotation	Nigerian Individuals and Institutional Investors	1,688,175	–	196,868	196,868	1,491,307	
8	NAL Merchant Bank Plc	Share Flotation	Nigerian Individuals and Institutional Investors	1,692,604		211,263	211,263	1,481,341	**8 and 9 combined**
9	International Merchant Bank Plc	Share Flotation	Nigerian Individuals and Institutional Investors	1,572,187					
10	Ashaka Cement Company Plc	Core Investor Sale	Bluecircle Industries Limited						
		Shares Sale	Individuals	558,426		178,671	178,671	1,951,942	
11	Nigerdock Nigeria Limited	Core Investor Sale	Global Energy Company Limited	5,130,675	98,327	137,542	235,869	4,894,806	

No.	Company	Type of Sale	Buyer						Notes
12	Assurance Bank Nigeria Plc	Core Investor Sale	Parmex/Gensec Consortium Ltd.	853,200	–	81,195	81,195	772,005	
13	Calabar Cement Company Ltd	Liquidation	Flour Mills & Holcim of Spain	216,081	–	10,359	10,359	205,722	
14	Capital Hotels Plc (Abuja Sheraton Hotel)	Core Investor Sale	Hans Gremlin Ltd.	4,303,087	–	77,760	77,760	4,225,327	
		Shares Sale	Nigerian Individuals and Institutional Investors						
15	Festac 77 Hotel	Asset Sale	UAC Properties Plc	1,010,000	136,311	50,287	186,598	823,402	
16	Nigeria Hotel Limited: Ikoyi Hotel Limited	Asset Sale	Beta Consortium	3,992,499	1,479,111	147,973	1,627,084	2,365,415	16–20 and 112 combined
17	Nigeria Hotel Limited: Caterers' Court, Lagos	Asset Sale	Reliance Estates						
18	Nigeria Hotel Limited Houses Nos 8 & 9, Leese Rd	Asset Sale	Chyzob Enterprises						

Table A3.2
(continued)

S/N	Transaction	Method of sale	Name of investor	Gross proceeds	Creditors/ staff payments	Other expenses	Total cost of sales	Net proceeds	Remarks
19	Nigeria Hotel Limited: Audit Section (Property), Lagos	Asset Sale	Dangote Group						
20	NPA Quarters, Lagos (NHL)	Asset Sale	Labana Glover Ventures						
21	Electricity Meter Company of Nigeria, Zaria	Core Investor Sale	Dantata Investments Ltd.	610,867	–	37,338	37,338	573,529	
22	Savannah Sugar Company Ltd.	Core Investor Sale 4.88% FGN Equity	Dangote IndLtd (Nig) Adamawa State Government	1,350,000	2,105,111	20,918	2,126,029	(776,029)	
23	National Trucks Manufacturers, Kano	Core Investor Sale	Art Engineering Limited	1,208,885	–	112,735	112,735	1,096,150	
24	Nigeria Reinsurance Corporation	Core Investor Sale	Reinsurance Acquisition Group	1,035,999	1,016,746	1,163,649	2,180,395	(1,144,396)	
25	West African Refinery Company Limited, Sierra Leone	Core Investor Sale	Majestic Oil Services Ltd	47,955	–	27,290	27,290	20,665	

26	Daily Times of Nigera Plc	Core Investor Sale	1,409,139	134,756	616,997	751,753	657,386
27	Peugeot Automobile Nigeria	Sale to existing shareholder	1,856,826	367,752	15,426	383,178	1,473,648
28	Ore-Irele Oil Palm	Core Investor Sale	160,020	22,005	11,634	33,639	126,381
29	Delta Steel Company Limited	Core Investor Sale	3,961,639	5,134,793	119,330	5,254,123	(1,292,484)
30	Leyland Nigeria Limited	Revalidation of Sale	274,015	—	98,680	98,680	175,335
31	Ikorodu Bricks and Clay	Core Investor Sale	306,000	—	5,231	5,231	300,769
32	Ibadan Bricks and Clay	Core Investor Sale	75,000	—	2,158	2,158	72,842
33	Enugu Bricks and Clay	Core Investor Sale	50,000	—	2,212	2,212	47,788
34	Kaduna Bricks and Clay	Core Investor Sale	51,000	—	2,158	2,158	48,842

Table A3.2
(continued)

S/N	Transaction	Method of sale	Name of investor	Gross proceeds	Creditors/ staff payments	Other expenses	Total cost of sales	Net proceeds	Remarks
35	Kano Bricks and Clay	Core Investor Sale	Associated Partners Limited	175,000	–	61	61	174,939	
36	Ihechiowa Oil Palm	Core Investor	Omen International Ltd	37,600	–	41,273	41,273	(3,673)	
37	Afribank Plc	Share Flotation	Various Individual and Institutional Investors	5,573,423	7,155	4,909,577	4,916,732	656,691	
38	Federal Superphospate Fertilizer Company	Core Investor Sale	HekioConsortium	777,694	343,611	49,481	393,092	384,602	
39	Nicon Hilton Hotel (NIRMSCO)	Core Investor Sale	Capital Consortium	13,602,750	–	69,527	69,527	13,533,223	
40	Nicon Insurance	Core Investor	Assurance Acquisition	8,499,951	3,876,006	1,168,099	5,044,105	3,455,846	
41	Volkswagen Nigeria Limited	Core Investor Sale	Barbedos Ventures	612,396	–	19,685	19,685	592,711	
42	Ayip-Eku Oil Palm	Core Investor Sale	Wingsong M-House Palm Oil Investment Ltd	566,621	33,943	19,200	53,143	513,478	

43	Nigerian Sugar Company, Bacita	Liquidation	Joseph Dam & Son	1,427,487	—	28,954	28,954	1,398,533
44	Oshogbo Steel Rolling Company Limited	Liquidation	Kura Holdings Limited	1,800,000	140,472	455,471	595,943	1,204,057
45	Jos Steel Rolling Mill	Liquidation	Zuma Steel West AfricaLimited					Proceeds w/ Liquidator
46	Katsina Steel Rolling Mill	Liquidation	Dana Holdings					Proceeds w/ Liquidator
47	National Aviation Handling Company	Public Offer of Sales at NSE	Various Individual and Institutional Investors	995,174	—	142,819	142,819	852,355
48	Eleme Petrochemicals Company Limited	Core Investor Sale	Indorama Group	32,463,679	17,028,188	50,795	17,078,983	15,384,696
49	Nigeria Machine Tools Ltd	Core Investor Sale	Bronwen Nigeria Ltd	1,000,000	222,444	23,165	245,609	754,391
50	Sunti Sugar	Liquidation	Dewo Integrated Farms Ltd	55,162	—	62,647	62,647	(7,485)
51	Nigeria Paper Mill, Jebba	Liquidation	IMNL Ltd	269,060	324,717	39,449	364,166	(95,106)
52	Abuja International Hotels Limited (Le-Meridian Hotel)	Core Investor	Hotel Acquisition Ltd	6,350,000	825,882	94,625	920,507	5,429,493

Table A3.2
(continued)

S/N	Transaction	Method of sale	Name of investor	Gross proceeds	Creditors/ staff payments	Other expenses	Total cost of sales	Net proceeds	Remarks
53	National Clearing and Forwarding Agency	Core Investor	Jorotom International Agency (Nigeria) Ltd	3,600,000	298,459	11,626	310,085	3,289,915	
54	Steyr Nigeria Ltd	Core Investor	Scintilla Prime Investment Ltd	800,000	–	244,012	244,012	555,988	
55	Igun Gold District (ML 20501, ML20507, ML10904)	Mineral Concession	Livinspring Minerals	30,954	–	–	–	30,954	**55–57 combined**
56	Nigeria Barytes Mining (ML 18706)	Mineral Concession	Emo Energy & Mining Company Ltd						
57	Nigeria Kaolin Package (ML5543, ML11930, ML5647, ML1939, M L4069)	Mineral Concession	Emo Energy & Mining Company Ltd						

No.	Description	Type	Company					58-63 combined
58	Nigeria FeldSpar/Quartzz (QLS2283, QLS2284, QLS2285, QL S2286) Lokoja	Mineral Concession	Livinspring Minerals	624,637	–	34,269	34,269	590,368
59	Nigeria Tin and Allied Mining & Product Ltd, Gurum Plateau	Mineral Concession	Equator Mines Ltd					
60	Nigeria Tin and Allied Mining & Product Titles Rafin Jaki, Bauchi State	Mineral Concession	Equator Mines Ltd					
61	Nigeria Tin and Allied Mining & Product Ltd, Gurum Banke Kaduna	Mineral Concession	Equator Mines Ltd					
62	ASEPL 202 (Lead, Zinc, Barytes, Copper, Salt (Og oja, Cross River)	Mineral Concession	Emo Energy & Mining Company ltd					
63	ASEPL 203 (Lead, Zinc, Barytes, Copper, Salt (Og oja, Cross River)	Mineral Concession	Emo Energy & Mining Company ltd					

Table A3.2
(continued)

S/N	Transaction	Method of sale	Name of investor	Gross proceeds	Creditors/ staff payments	Other expenses	Total cost of sales	Net proceeds	Remarks
64	Anambra Motor Manufacturing Company Limited (ANAMMCO)	Core Investor	G. U. OKEKE & SONs	773,667	–	30,326	30,326	743,341	
65	Central Packaging Limited	Core Investor	Gobesh (W.A.) Ltd	114,850	79,657	19,509	99,166	15,684	
66	Nigeria Newsprint Manufacturing Company Ltd	Liquidation	Negris Holdings Ltd	400,000	37,930	37,728	75,658	324,342	
67	Stallion House, V. I. Lagos	Core Investor	Luzon Oil & Gas Limited	2,210,000	102,491	18,007	120,498	2,089,502	
68	Baker Nigeria Limited	Private Placement	Baker Hughes Nigeria Limited	53,491	–	3,110	3,110	50,381	
69	Baroid Drilling Chemical Products Nigeria Limited	Private Placement	Geofluids- Limited/Glad Company Limited	88,656	–	5,069	5,069	83,587	
		Sale of staff shares	BDCPL						
70	Baroid of Nigeria Limited	Private Placement	Halliburton Operations Nigeria Ltd	156,198	–	8,833	8,833	147,365	

	Company	Investor	Method					
71	Dowell Schlumberger Nigeria Limited	Bussdor & Company Limited	Private Placement	648,000	–	36,238	36,238	611,762
72	M-I Nigeria Limited	AP Oilfield Services Limited	Private Placement	345,296	–	19,370	19,370	325,926
73	Schlumberger Testing & Production Services Nigeria Limited	ABB ELS	Private Placement	64,080	–	3,699	3,699	60,381
74	Sedco Forex of Nigeria Limited	Frazimex Nigeria Ltd	Private Placement	518,400	–	29,016	29,016	489,384
75	Solus Schall Nigeria Limited	Baklang Consultants	Private Placement	12,034	–	800	800	11,234
76	Aluminium Smelter Company of Nigeria Ltd	RUSAL	Core Investor Sale	16,665,536	4,374,948	341,543	4,716,491	11,949,045
77	Izom Bricks	Continental Projects Development and Supply Ltd	Core Investor	50,000	–	18 / 19,310	18 / 19,310	49,982 / 1,761,685
78	Onigbolo Cement Company	Dangote Group of Companies	Core Investor	1,780,995	–	2,673	2,673	1,419,549
79	LPG Calabar Depot	Sahara Energy Resources Ltd	Asset sale	1,422,222	–			

Table A3.2
(continued)

S/N	Transaction	Method of sale	Name of investor	Gross proceeds	Creditors/ staff payments	Other expenses	Total cost of sales	Net proceeds	Remarks
80	EPL 1400 (Gold Waya, Yauri, Kebbi)	Mineral Concession	Equator Mine Ltd	196,044	–	–	–	196,044	80–84 combined
81	EPL 13212 (Talc, Gold, Cassiterite, Atakumosa,	Concession	Shoreline Power Co. Ltd						
82	EPL 17222 (Gold Bukkuyyum LG	Mineral Concession	Western Metal Products company Ltd						
83	EPL 17224 Gold Bukkuyyum LG	Mineral Concession	Western Metal Products company Ltd						
84	EPL 17227 (Gold Bukkuyyum LG	Mineral Concession	Western Metal Products company Ltd						
85	Okaba Coal Block (NCC)	Concession	Denca Services Ltd	3,294,235	–	25,290	25,290	3,268,945	80–84 combined
86	Ogboyega North (NCC)	Concession	Western Metal Products Co. Ltd						
87	Ogboyega South (NCC)	Concession	Western Metal Products Co. Ltd						
88	Lafiagi Sugar Company Ltd	Liquidation	BUA International Ltd	11,111	–	17,151	17,151	(6,040)	

		Core Investor					
89	Flour Mills		6,240	–	1,099	1,099	5,141
90	United Nig. Insurance		17,568	–	1,371	1,371	16,197
91	Niyamco		3,213	–	620	620	2,593
92	Niger, NEM, WAPIC		8,548	–	1,028	1,028	7,520
93	BAICO, Law Union, Guinea, UNLIC		12,904	–	844	844	12,060
94	AIICO, REAN, Prestige, Sun Insurance		29,152	–	1,543	1,543	27,609
95	Okomu Oil Palm		23,106	–	1,518	1,518	21,588
96	ABATEX		18,002	–	1,413	1,413	16,589
97	National Salt Plc		9,877	–	646	646	9,231
98	Impresit Bakolori		5,880	–	983	983	4,897
99	First Bank of Nigeria Plc		187,407	–	4,863	4,863	182,544
100	Union Bank of Nigeria Plc		262,467	–	48,567	48,567	213,900
101	Savannah Bank Plc		51,007	–	4,408	4,408	46,599
102	UBA Plc		164,750	–	11,041	11,041	153,709

Table A3.2
(continued)

S/N	Transaction	Method of sale	Name of investor	Gross proceeds	Creditors/ staff payments	Other expenses	Total cost of sales	Net proceeds	Remarks
103	Allied Bank Plc			14,383	–	1,925	1,925	12,458	
104	Niger Cement			187,270	–	11,852	11,852	175,418	
105	MV Abuja			441,550	3,511	57,892	61,403	380,177	
106	Nigerian Unity Line			2,600,975	103,896	22,415	126,311	2,474,664	
107	Egbin Power Plant Plc			3,584,000	–	98	98	3,583,902	
108	NITEL/MTEL			63,030,000	63,183,118	2,263,098	65,446,216	(2,416,216)	
109	Nigerian Paper Mill, Iwopin			855,000	56,520	13,313	69,833	785,167	
110	Bitumen Blocks I & II			418,080	–	9,658	9,658	408,422	
111	BAKER HUGHES NIGERIA LIMITED			43,765	–	2,568	2,568	41,197	
112	Central Hotel, Kano	Asset Sale	Broadfields & Asset Mgt						
113	NICON shares in Niger Insurance—2002			621,428				621,428	
A				235,027,083	102,205,893	19,197,814	121,403,707	113,623,406	

ADJUSTMENT FOR PRE-1999 PROCEEDS

1	National Oil & Chemical Marketing Co. Plc (now CONOIL Plc)	35,339
2	African Petroleum Plc	32,832
3	Cement Company of Northern Nigeria Plc	72,000
4	Ashaka Cement Company Plc	39,000
5	Benue Cement Co. Plc	42,607
6	Unipetrol Nigeria Plc	96,000
7	NAL / IMB Merchant Bank Plc	172,193
8	F S B International Bank Plc	85,034
9	Flour Mills	6,240

Table A3.2
(continued)

S/N	Transaction	Method of sale	Name of investor	Gross proceeds	Creditors/ staff payments	Other expenses	Total cost of sales	Net proceeds	Remarks
10	United Nigeria Insurance			17,568					
11	Niyamco			3,213					
12	Niger, NEM, WAPIC			8,548					
13	BAICO, Law Union, Guinea, UNLIC			12,904					
14	AIICO, REAN, Prestige, Sun Insurance			29,152					
15	Okomu Oil Palm			23,106					
16	Ayip Eku Oil Palm			5,921					
17	ABATEX			18,002					
18	National Salt Plc			9,877					
19	Impresit Bakolori Plc			5,880					
20	First Bank of Nigeria Plc			187,407					
21	Afribank Plc			264,453					
22	Union Bank Plc			262,467					

23	Savannah Bank Plc	51,007				
24	United Bank for Africa Plc	164,750				
25	Allied Bank Plc	14,383				
		1,659,883				
B	PROCEEDS AFTER PRE-1999 ADJUSTMENT CONCESSIONS	233,367,200	102,205,893	19,197,814	121,403,707	111,963,493
1	APAPA CONTAINER TERMINAL	1,285,000	1,069,692	77,546	1,147,238	137,762
2	APAPA TERMINAL 'A' PORT	1,655,262	529,558	34,684	564,242	1,091,020
3	APAPA TERMINAL 'B PORT	128,500	117,492	6,923	124,415	4,085
4	APAPA TERMINAL 'C' PORT	309,989	266,267	21,207	287,474	22,515
5	APAPA TERMINAL 'D' PORT	2,478,443	217,742	13,742	231,484	2,246,959
6	APAPA TERMINAL 'E' PORT	385,500	329,110	21,615	350,725	34,775

Table A3.2
(continued)

S/N	Transaction	Method of sale	Name of investor	Gross proceeds	Creditors/ staff payments	Other expenses	Total cost of sales	Net proceeds	Remarks
7	OTHER TERMINALS & PORT			4,692,198	1,091,170	72,625	1,163,795	3,528,403	
8	CALABAR TERMINAL 'B' PORT			12,850	22,053	1,633	23,686	(10,836)	
9	ONNER FED. LIGHTER TERMINAL			386,993	329,906	22,912	352,818	34,175	
10	PORT HARCOURT TERMINAL 'A'			297,187	224,106	14,103	238,209	58,978	
11	PORT HARCOURT TERMINAL 'B'			167,393	117,511	7,260	124,771	42,622	
12	WARRI OLD TERMINAL'B'			12,799	10,369	733	11,102	1,697	
13	TINCAN TERMINAL 'A'			263,482	228,084	14,049	242,133	21,349	
14	TINCAN TERMINAL 'B'			1,339,412	694,237	44,918	739,155	600,257	
15	TINCAN TERMINAL 'C'			1,012,110	224,106	13,756	237,862	774,248	
16	TINCAN RORO TERMINAL			411,600	350,588	21,754	372,342	39,258	

17	ABUJA INTL' AIRPORT	1,273,350		14,370	14,370	1,258,980
18	LAGOS INTERN TRADE FAIR	212,731		38,467	38,467	174,264
19	KOKO PORT TERMINAL	21,823		47	47	21,776
20	TINCAN LILYPOND INLAND CONT.	64,000		140	140	63,860
21	WARRI CARNAL TERMINAL 'B'	12,799		34	34	12,765
22	CALABAR NEW TERM. 'A'	31,499		119	119	31,380
23	CALABAR NEW TERM 'B'	31,996		–		31,996
24	CALABAR OLD TERM	12,800		–		12,800
25	WARRI OLD TERM 'A'	1,356		–		1,356
26	WARI NEW TERM 'A'	94		34	34	60
27	WARRI NEW TERM 'B'	100,250	147,884	34	34	100,216
28	TAFAWA BALEWA SQUARE	150,000		16,073	163,957	(13,957)
C		16,751,416	5,969,875	458,778	6,428,653	10,322,763

Table A3.2
(continued)

S/N	Transaction	Method of sale	Name of investor	Gross proceeds	Creditors/staff payments	Other expenses	Total cost of sales	Net proceeds	Remarks
	CORE INVESTORS SALE & PUBLIC OFFERS			233,367,200	102,205,893	19,197,814	121,403,707	111,963,493	SEE 'C'
	CONCESSIONS			16,751,416	5,969,875	458,778	6,428,653	10,322,763	
	TOTAL			250,118,616	108,175,768	19,656,592	127,832,360	122,286,256	APPENDIX A
	2010								
	Savannah Sugar			110,176				110,176	
	Sundry Expenses						830,270	(830,270)	
	2011								
	Capita Hotel	Sale of shares		237,796				237,796	
	Ndionuoha Fish Farm	Core Investor		300				300	
	Baroid Drilling Chemical Products Nig. Ltd	Sale of shares		9,850				9,850	
	EPCL share sale to staff-2001			975,000				975,000	
	Sundry Expenses						174,191	(174,191)	APPENDIX A
	TOTAL			251,451,738	108,175,768	19,656,592	128,836,821	122,614,917	
	NET RECEIPTS							25,164,199	SEE 'D'
	GRAND TOTAL			251,451,738	108,175,768	19,656,592	128,836,821	147,779,116	

Table A5.1
Giving stolen money back to the people: use of repatriated Abacha funds. Source: Okonjo-Iweala 2007b, p. 9.

Sector	Allocation[a] (billions of naira)	Funds accounted for via Projects List (billions of naira)
Power	21.07	21.94
Rural electrification		8.10
Power generation		13.84
Works	18.60	17.06
Priority economic roads		
Health	10.83	10.84
Primary health care		2.02
Vaccination programs		8.82
Basic and secondary education	7.74	7.79
Primary schools		3.16
Junior secondary schools		3.40
Federal govt. colleges		1.23
Water	6.20	7.53
Potable water and rural irrigation		
Total	65.07	65.16

a. Based on preliminary information.

Table A6.1
Milestones in Nigeria's journey into and out of debt, 1964–2007.

1964	Nigeria takes its first Paris Club loan (for US$13.1 million).
1973–1981	Oil boom leads to a substantial windfall for Nigeria.
1982	Oil-price crash begins; interest rates rise substantially.
1985	External debt has risen to US$19 billion from US$1.3 billion in 1976. Debt service has climbed to US$4 billion per year; Nigeria is able to pay only US$1.5 billion.
September 1986	Nigeria floats the naira. The black-market premium on foreign exchange is 400 percent.
1986	First Paris Club rescheduling.
1991	Agreement reached with commercial creditors of London Club to consolidate and treat private debt arrears and obligations under Brady Plan.
Mid 1990s	Paris Club relationship hits a low under dictator Abacha as Nigeria suspends debt servicing.
1998	New government of General Abdulsalam Abubakar tries to restore goodwill by making payment of US$1.5 billion to Paris Club.
1999	Democratically elected President Olusegun Obasanjo puts debt issue at center stage as he campaigns for debt relief.
2000	Author invited by President Obasanjo to sort out Nigeria's tangled debt situation; seven different agencies managed debt. Debt Management Office established.
July 17, 2003	Author sworn in as Nigeria's Minister of Finance in charge of development and implementation of homegrown reform program, NEEDS.
September and October 2003	Presentation to UK Chancellor of the Exchequer Gordon Brown on the preliminary outline of Nigeria's proposed reform program and beginning of getting his buy-in
2004	Oil Price-based Fiscal Rule adopted.
December 31, 2004	Nigeria's external debt stands at US$35.994 billion (of which 86 percent, or US$30.9 billion, is owed to the Paris Club).
February and March 2005	Early presentation to Paris Club.
May 5, 2005	Author and President Obasanjo visit White House seeking President Bush's support.
May 29, 2005	Gordon Brown supports Nigeria's request for debt relief and negotiates debt-relief terms with G8 finance ministers at their May meeting.
Mid June–June 29, 2005	Debt diplomacy with non-G8 Paris Club creditors.
June 29, 2005	Nigeria and Paris Club reach historic 60 percent debt write-off agreement in principle on basis of terms discussed at G8 meeting, but subject to IMF's blessing of Nigeria's homegrown program.

Table A6.1
(continued)

July 8, 2005	G8 heads of state bless Nigeria's debt-relief proposal.
September 2005	Nigeria becomes the first country whose homegrown program
October 3, 2005	is encapsulated in a Policy Support Instrument. Policy Support Instrument is submitted for approval by IMF Board.
October 18 and 19, 2005	Non-stop negotiations with Paris Club.
October 2005– March 2006	Debt write-off implemented in three stages.
March and April 2006	Nigeria pays final installment on its Paris Club debt.
November 2007	President Shehu Musa Yar'Adua signs Fiscal Responsibility Bill.

Table A6.2

A weak foundation: Nigeria's economic indicators, 1992–2002 (annual percentage change). Source: Federal Government of Nigeria, unpublished data.

	1992	1993	1994	1995	1996	1997	1998	1999	2000	2001	2002
TotalGDP	2.43	0.58	-1.61	2.29	6.2	2.77	0.23	1.49	5.64	3.31	1.42
OilGDP	2.27	1.24	0.12	2.17	4.48	1.47	-5.39	-4.13	11.54	1.42	-11.63
Non-oilGDP	2.52	0.21	-2.58	2.35	7.17	3.51	3.4	4.39	2.84	4.28	7.96
Consumerpriceindexa	48.8	61.3	76.8	51.6	14.3	10.2	11.9	0.2	14.5	16.5	12.2

a. Year-on-year inflation.

Table A6.3
Improving fundamentals: Nigeria's economic indicators, 2002–2006 (annual percentage change). Source: Federal Government of Nigeria, unpublished data.

Indicator	2002	2003	2004	2005	2006
Real GDP (at 1990 factor cost)	1.42	10.9	6.1	6.2	5.7
Oil GDP	–11.63	26.5	3.5	2.6	–4.5
Non-oil GDP	7.96	4.4	7.4	8.2	8.9
Inflation rate (year-on-year)	12.2	21.80	10.00	11.60	8.5
External reserves (US$ billion)	7.7	7.5	17.0	28.3	43.8

Table A6.4
Targets for servicing debt: debt sustainability indicators for Nigeria, 2004 and 2015. Sources: IMF and World Bank 2004; World Bank 2005.

Indicator	World Bank–IMF debt-sustainability-framework benchmark	2004 Nigeria (actual)	2015 projected baseline	2015 projected (with oil-price shock)[a]
Net present value of debt as percent of GDP	30	48.8	21.9	70
Net present value of debt as percent of exports	100	90.4	46.1	211
Net present value of debt as percent of revenue, excluding grants	200	114.5	58.9	NA[b]
Debt service as percent of exports	15	7.5	3.9	NA
Debt service as percent of revenue	20	12.9	6.4	NA

a. Assumes a permanent reduction in oil prices of $16 per barrel equivalent to 2 standard deviations of Brent oil prices for period 1976–2004.
b. Not available.

Notes

Chapter 1

1. Nigerian National Petroleum Corporation, "NNPC and the Nigerian Oil and Gas Industry: Looking towards the Future. A Corporate Profile of the NNPC," June 2008.

2. The term "Dutch Disease" refers to the repercussions to an economy of a sharp and/or sudden rise in the inflow of foreign currency, resulting from—for example—the discovery and exploration of natural resources such as oil or precious metals. The currency inflows lead to currency appreciation, making the country's other products (usually in the agriculture and manufacturing sectors) less price-competitive on the export market. As a result, productivity in these other sectors declines rapidly, and their contribution to national income falls. The term was coined in 1977 by *The Economist* to describe the decline of the manufacturing sector in the Netherlands after the discovery (in 1959) and exportation of large quantities of natural gas. See Ebrahim-zadeh 2003.

3. Nigerian National Planning Commission 2004, p. viii.

Chapter 3

1. See Adam Smith International 2005.

2. This section draws on PowerPoint presentations and data provided by the Bureau of Public Enterprises, including a speech by Irene Chigbue, Director General of Bureau of Public Enterprises, on March 5, 2007.

3. See Chigbue 2007.

Chapter 4

1. This section draws on Okonjo-Iweala and Osafo-Kwaako 2007.

Chapter 5

1. See Swiss Federal Court Decision of February 7, 2005, Public Law Court 1, Presiding Judge Feraud.

2. BBC News (http://news.bbc.co.uk), "Nigeria Probes Siemens Bribe Case," November 21, 2007.

3. See for example, *Financial Times* (http://www.ft.com), "Nigeria Gas Consortium 'Evasive', Says Probe Chief," August 23, 2004.

4. The annual Transparency International Corruption Perceptions Index (CPI), the first of which was released in 1995, ranks more than 150 countries by their perceived levels of corruption as determined by expert assessments and opinion surveys. It has been widely credited with putting Transparency International and the issue of corruption on the international policy agenda. See http://www.transparency.org/policy_research/surveys_indices/cpi/2009

5. See Kaufmann, Kraay, and Mastruzzi 2009.

Chapter 6

1. The loan was for $13.1 million, from the Italian government, for the construction of the Niger dam.

2. See Okonjo-Iweala, Soludo, and Muhtar 2003.

3. Pinto 1987, pp. 431–435.

4. Under this plan, Nigeria obtained 60 percent debt relief on 62 percent of its US$5.8 billion London Club obligations by executing a buy-back at 40 cents on the dollar. The remaining US$2.04 billion was collateralized with US zero coupon bonds maturing in 2002.

5. The International Development Association is the arm of the World Bank that is designed to help the poorest countries in the world. It lends money (known as credits) on concessional terms. This means that IDA credits have no interest charge and repayments are stretched over 35 to 40 years, including a 10-year grace period. The IDA also provides grants to countries at risk of debt distress.

6. The IMF team included Menachem Katz (Mission Leader), Idrisa Thiam (Resident Representative), Calvin McDonald, Jeanne Gobat, Ulrich Bartsch, L. Nielsen, Mauricio Villafuerte, and others. The World Bank team included Hafez Ghanem (Country Director), Victoria Kwakwa (Lead Economist), and others.

7. The Group of Twenty-Four countries are Algeria, Argentina, Brazil, Colombia, Côte d'Ivoire, the Democratic Republic of Congo, Egypt, Ethiopia, Gabon, Ghana, Guatemala, India, Iran, Lebanon, Mexico, Nigeria, Peru, South Africa, Trinidad and Tobago, Pakistan, the Philippines, Sri Lanka, Syria, and Venezuela.

8. The HIPC Initiative was launched in 1996 and enhanced in 1999. To date, 35 low-income countries have qualified for debt relief and another five countries are potentially eligible. The total cost of HIPC Initiative debt relief to creditors is estimated at US$74 billion in end-2008 net-present-value terms.

9. Source: letter from Jon Cunliffe, Managing Director, Macroeconomic Policy and International Finance, HM Treasury, to Anne Krueger, First Deputy Managing Director, IMF, and Shengman Zhang, Managing Director, World Bank, March 9, 2005.

10. This baseline study found that fiscal policy was consistent with a non-oil primary deficit of 40 percent of non-oil GDP, which was compatible with a fiscal rule fixing the non-oil primary deficit at a reference oil price of US$25 per barrel in 2002 prices. The baseline computed oil revenues using the IMF's World Economic Outlook (WEO) forecast, which stated that oil prices averaged US$46.5 per barrel for 2005 and would decline

gradually to US$33 per barrel in 2016, after which they would grow at 2 percent per year. Since interest payments on debt are fixed, the focus was on the non-oil fiscal deficit excluding these payments (known in technical language as the non-oil primary deficit).

11. The US$4 decline is equal to half a standard deviation of the fluctuations in the prices of Brent crude oil from 1976 to 2004.

12. Fifty percent of this 72 percent was external debt; the remaining 22 percent was domestic T-bills and bonds and arrears.

13. In his working paper titled Anatomy of a 2005 Debt Deal: Nigeria and the Paris Club, Thomas Callaghy (2007, p. 29) quotes Ann Pettifor, leader of the Jubilee campaign, as describing the World Bank report as "vital in the final stages of this complex geo-political exercise."

14. Speech to the Abuja Conference on Debt Reduction, May 17, 2001.

15. This was a term I coined in 2000 for President Obasanjo to use in his lobbying effort, as described in chapter 1. He used it often, to great effect.

16. The non-G8 members are Austria, Belgium, Denmark, Finland, the Netherlands, Spain, and Switzerland.

17. Thomas Callaghy notes this irony in the conclusion of his 2007 working paper.

Chapter 8

1. See, for instance, Okonjo-Iweala 2009 and Okonjo-Iweala 2011.

2. See Treichel 2011.

3. Standard & Poors downgraded the credit rating of the United States from AAA to AA+ in August of 2011.

4. See http://www.doingbusiness.org/

5. See http://www.transparency.org/policy_research/surveys_indices/cpi

References

Adegoroye, G. 2006. Public Service Reform for Sustainable Development: The Nigerian Experience. Keynote address, Commonwealth Advanced Seminar, Wellington, New Zealand.

Adam Smith International. 2005. Economic Policy Positioning Paper 7, Bureau of Public Enterprises.

BPE (Bureau of Public Enterprises). 2007a. Report on Ports Terminals Concession Monitoring—Portharcourt, Warri, and Calabar Ports, February.

BPE (Bureau of Public Enterprises). 2007b. PowerPoint presentations and data, including a speech by Irene Chigbue, Director General of BPE, March 5.

Budina, Nina, Gaobo Pang, and Sweder van Wijnbergen. 2007. Nigeria's Growth Record: Dutch Disease or Debt Overhang? Policy Research Working Paper 4256, World Bank, Washington.

Callaghy, Thomas. 2007. Anatomy of a 2005 Debt Deal: Nigeria and the Paris Club. Working paper, Political Science Department, University of Pennsylvania.

Chigbue, Irene. 2007. Nigerian Privatization Program—The Journey So Far. Bureau of Public Enterprises.

Ebrahim-Zadeh, Christine. 2003. Back to Basics—Dutch Disease: Too Much Wealth Managed Unwisely. *Finance and Development* 40, no.1 (http://www.imf.org/external/pubs/ft/fandd/2003/03/ebra.htm).

Governments of the Netherlands and Belgium. 2011. Mutual Interests—Mutual Benefits: Evaluation of the 2005 Debt Relief Agreement between the Paris Club and Nigeria. Summary Report, March.

International Monetary Fund (IMF). 2001. Nigeria: 2001 Article IV Consultation. Country Report 01/131, International Monetary Fund, Washington.

International Monetary Fund (IMF). 2003. Nigeria: 2002 Article IV Consultation. IMF Country Report 03/3, International Monetary Fund, Washington.

International Monetary Fund (IMF). 2005. *Nigeria: Selected Issues and Statistical Appendix.*

International Monetary Fund (IMF). 2006a. First Review under the Policy Support Instrument.

International Monetary Fund (IMF). 2006b. *Integrating Poor Countries into the World Trading System.*

Kaufmann, Daniel. 2005. "Nigeria in Numbers–The Governance Dimension. A Preliminary and Brief Review of Recent Trends on Governance and Corruption. Presentation for the President of Nigeria and His Economic Management Team, World Bank, Washington.

Kaufmann, Daniel, Aart Kraay, and Massimo Mastruzzi. 2009. *Governance Matters 2009: Worldwide Governance Indicators, 1996–2008* (http://info.worldbank.org/governance/wgi/).

Nigerian National Petroleum Corporation (NNPC). 2008. NNPC and the Nigerian Oil and Gas Industry: Looking towards the future. A corporate profile of the NNPC. June.

Nigerian National Planning Commission. 2004. Meeting Everyone's Needs: National Economic Empowerment and Development Strategy.

Okonjo-Iweala, Ngozi. 2007a. Corruption: Myths and Realities in a Developing Country Context. Richard H. Sabot Lecture, Center for Global Development, Washington.

Okonjo-Iweala, Ngozi. 2007b. Stolen Assets Recovery Initiative: The Nigerian Experience. Working paper, World Bank, Washington.

Okonjo-Iweala, Ngozi. 2009. Global Financial Crisis: Impact and Implications for Nigeria. Presentation at African University of Science and Technology, Abuja, Nigeria.

Okonjo-Iweala, Ngozi. 2011. Securing a Diversified Economic Future for Nigeria. In *Half a Century of Progress and Challenges*, ed. Constance Chiogor Ikokwu. True Expressions.

Okonjo-Iweala, Ngozi, and Philip Osafo-Kwaako. 2007. Nigeria's Economic Reforms: Progress and Challenges. Global Working Paper 6, Brookings Institution.

Okonjo-Iweala, Ngozi, Charles Soludo, and Mansur Muhtar. 2003. *The Debt Trap in Nigeria: Towards a Sustainable Debt Strategy.* Africa World Press.

Organization of Petroleum Exporting Countries (OPEC). 2011. *Annual Statistical Bulletin*, 2010–2011 edition.

Pinto, Brian. 1987. Nigeria During and After the Oil Boom: A Policy Comparison with Indonesia. *World Bank Economic Review* 1 (3): 419–445.

Pinto, Brian. 2005. Nigeria's Opportunity of a Generation: Meeting the MDGs, Reducing Indebtedness. Report prepared for Africa Region, World Bank, Washington.

Sanusi, Sanusi Lamido. 2010. The Nigerian Banking Industry: What Went Wrong and the Way Forward. Lecture at Annual Convocation Ceremony, Bayero University, Kano.

Schiavo-Campo, Salvatore, and P. S. A. Sundaram. 2001. *To Serve and to Preserve: Improving Public Administration in a Competitive World.* Asian Development Bank.

Treichel, Volker, ed. 2010. *Putting Nigeria to Work: A Strategy for Employment and Growth.* World Bank.

Transparency International. Various years. Corruption Perception Index. http://www.transparency.org/policy_research/surveys_indices/cpi/2009

World Bank. 1981. *Nigeria Basic Economic Report.*

World Bank. 2003. NIGERIA: Policy Options for Growth and Stability. Report 26215-NGA.

World Bank. 2005. *The Economic Policy and Debt Department Note on Fiscal Sustainability for Oil-rich Developing Countries.* World Bank.

World Bank. Various years. Worldwide Governance Indicators (WGI). http://info .worldbank.org/governance/wgi/

About the Author

Dr. Ngozi Okonjo-Iweala is currently Nigeria's Coordinating Minister for the Economy and Minister of Finance. From December 2007 to August 2011 she was Managing Director of the World Bank (the number-two position at the World Bank), where she had oversight responsibility for the World Bank's operational portfolio in Africa, in South Asia, and in Europe and Central Asia. Dr. Okonjo-Iweala spearheaded several World Bank initiatives to assist low-income countries during the food crisis and later during the financial crisis. In 2010 she chaired the World Bank's successful drive to raise $49.3 billion in grants and low-interest credit for the poorest countries in the world.

From September 2006 to November 2007, she was Distinguished Visiting Fellow at the Brookings Institution in Washington. Before that, she was Nigeria's Minister of Finance for three years and was briefly Minister of Foreign Affairs. As Minister of Finance, she spearheaded negotiations with the Paris Club of Creditors that led to the wiping out US$30 billion of Nigeria's debt, including the outright cancellation of 60 percent of Nigeria's external debt, equivalent to US$18 billion.

Before serving as Minister of Finance, Dr. Okonjo-Iweala had a 21-year career at the World Bank as a development economist, rising to the position of Vice President and Corporate Secretary in 2002.

Dr. Okonjo-Iweala is a member or chair of numerous boards and advisory groups, including the ONE Campaign, the Rockefeller Foundation, the African Institutes of Science and Technology, and the Center for Global Development. She has served on the advisory board of the Clinton Global Initiative and as an adviser to several international investment groups working in emerging markets. She has lectured extensively all over the world on development issues, especially those concerning Africa.

Dr. Okonjo-Iweala was the founder of Nigeria's first indigenous opinion-research organization, NOI-Gallup Polls. She founded the Center for the Study of Economies of Africa, a development research think tank based in Abuja, Nigeria's capital city.

She is a member of the Danish-government-led Commission on Africa, of the World Economic Forum Global Leadership Council on Transparency and Corruption, and of the Commission on World Growth.

Dr. Okonjo-Iweala was educated at Harvard University and has a PhD in regional economics and development from the Massachusetts Institute of Technology. She is the recipient of numerous awards, including the President of the Italian Republic Gold Medal by the Pia Manzu Centre in 2011, has been awarded honorary doctorates by Trinity College Dublin, Brown University, Amherst College, Colby College, and the Universities of Port Harcourt, Calabar, Obafemi Awolowo, and Abia State in Nigeria, among others. She has been ranked among the Top 100 Women in the World (*Forbes* and *The Guardian*, 2011), among the Top 150 Women in the World (*Newsweek*, 2011), among the Top 10 Most Influential Women in Africa (*Forbes*, 2011), among the Top 100 Most Inspiring People in the World Delivering for Girls and Women (Women Deliver, 2011), among 73 "brilliant" business influencers in the world by the *Condé Nast International Business Intelligence Magazine*, and among the Top 100 Global Thinkers of 2011 by *Foreign Policy*. In 2011 she received the Global Leadership Award from Chicago Council on Global Affairs. She is married and has four grown children.

Index